Barnhouse, Donald

Is anybody up there?

153035

DATE			

Donald Barnhouse

IS ANYBODY UP THERE?

Santa Claus, Flying Saucers and God

A Crossroad Book

THE SEABURY PRESS | NEW YORK

1977
The Seabury Press
815 Second Avenue
New York, N.Y. 10017

Printed in the United States of America
Designed by Victoria Gomez

Library of Congress Cataloging In Publication Data

Barnhouse, Donald, 1927–
  Is anybody up there?

  "A Crossroad book."
  1. Apologetics—20th century. I. Title.
BT1102.B26   239   76-51734   ISBN 0-8164-0305-8

Acknowledgments

First, to start with something obvious, I acknowledge that this book is not thorough. I thought it better to say something briefly in a first offering, perhaps writing at greater length later if the response to what is said here indicates interest.

Second, I acknowledge that the book is not original. At least it is not intended to be original in the sense that a new scientific theory should be original. Those who have read widely will recognize allusions to, and rephrasings of, the work of others. This means that doing a proper job of acknowledging would mean writing a kind of spiritual and intellectual autobiography, for which there is no conspicuous demand. So I'll just mention some of the strongest influences briefly.

Through my mother and father I received an appreciation of the joy of learning and understanding, and a strong awareness of how rich and varied a source the Bible is. I am particularly grateful to my mother for her almost incredibly warm and happy personality and for encouraging me to listen for the voice of God as Eli told Samuel to listen, without assuming that it must come through organizational channels. I am similarly grateful to my father for the fearlessness of his faith, and for telling me not to follow in his footsteps but to try to know God for myself and follow those larger footsteps directly.

My brother and sisters have had important parts also, and I managed to coerce my psychiatrist sister, Dr. Ruth Barnhouse, into reading the manuscript. Her counsel was brilliant and helpful, as usual; but as to the result, in the words of one of her favorite books, "No blame."

Also without holding them in any way responsible for what I have done with their offerings, I would like to acknowledge the numerous insights and the support at critical moments given me by a host of

ACKNOWLEDGMENTS

teachers, friends, and authors, starting with my two best friends, my daughters Margaret and Ruth. From the years at Princeton Theological Seminary I think particularly of John Mackay, George Hendry, Hans Hoffman, Paul Louis Lehman, and Otto Piper. For lessons learned in less formal settings, I will never forget Henrietta Mears, Dick Halverson, Cindy Walker, Paul Hewitt and Connie, Sidlow Baxter, Carl Anderson, Ralph Lingle, Gordon Meeks, and many more. Dr. Henry Brenman gave me strength through encouragement at a time when I needed it most. There is also another, who knows her part, though her name is very sadly gone from me.

In a unique place is Billy Graham, who gave me the privilege of working for him for a little over three years. I wish I could claim to have learned the lesson offered by his life, which shows an extraordinary and impressive consistency with his words and beliefs, even to those who work most closely with him.

A few authors have done me immense service by stimulating my thought, as my friends have, even though they often did not fully convince me. This provocative group includes Dietrich Bonhoeffer, Emil Brunner, Albert Camus, Nels Ferre, Karen Horney, Carl Jung, and B. F. Skinner. Unique among these literary tutors is C. S. Lewis, whose *Perelandra* did for me what he said George Macdonald's *Phantastes* did for him: it "baptized my imagination." Lewis made me a citizen of Narnia, a lover of Aslan, and one of the host of his grateful disciples. I deeply regret not writing this book in time to ask his counsel before publishing it, and I look for the day when I may meet him in that place where he dreamed that we might all become "solid people."

iv

Introduction

There's a story about a man who climbed a very steep and difficult mountain only to slip at the last moment and find himself sliding toward a thousand-foot fall. Reaching out frantically for something to hold onto, he caught a small scrubby bush that kept him from dropping, but he couldn't climb back up. In desperation he looked up to the sky and called, "Is anybody up there who can help me?"

Somewhat to his surprise a voice came back, and it said: "I can help you, but first you must let go of that bush." A long, quiet moment went by, and then the man called out again. "Is there anybody *else* up there who can help me?"

It's really a very serious question. The world is divided into people who hold the "nobody up there" view, several competing groups of people who are sure there is "only One up there," some who think there are "many up there," and a growing number who have given up trying to find the answer to the question, for all practical purposes taking the "nobody" view. A few, trying to dress the question up, say something to the effect that "really, in a sense a bit of all of us is up there!" But that really misses the point and we would simply have to start over from that level and ask whether there was anybody UP THERE, higher than ourselves.

You have probably heard of the famous newspaper column headed "Yes, Virginia, There Is a Santa Claus," written decades ago to a little girl who was troubled when her faith in that generous and lovable higher power was threatened. But for those who have outgrown both the faith in Santa Claus and the disappointment of losing that faith, as well as for those who are reluctant to let go of their particular bushes even though not happy just hanging on, what is the real answer to the question of whether there is anybody up there? And how can we seriously go about finding that answer?

Contents

CONTENTS

Section I

A Section Designed to Clear Some Religious and Secular Cobwebs by Pointing to a Few Similarities and Differences between *Santa Claus, Flying Saucers, and God*

You Have Your Concept of God
and I Have Mine

The popularity of Santa Claus is astonishing, despite the fact that no one in his right mind is supposed to believe in him. In one form or another he is almost universally loved around the world, even in places where the Christian religion is almost completely without followers. In Japan, only one percent of the people identify themselves as Christian, but the spirit of Santa Claus, of jollity and gift-giving, has made Christmas a time for children to look forward to there as well as in "Christian" nations.

Even here it is often that spirit of Santa Claus which plays a larger role in the sense of excitement and joy surrounding Christmas than any strong feelings about the Incarnation. Take a survey for yourself and check. Santa has a deep hold on people. Who could dislike him? He is always smiling, always giving, and those are lovable qualities. Maybe his strength and longevity derive in part from the fact that he is the object of such a great outpouring of love every winter, year after year. And he is almost never feared.

God is not so fortunate. I remember very well as a child being afraid of God. I have a vague memory of adult heads nodding in solemn approval when someone reading the Bible came to the passage where Solomon says: "The fear of the Lord is the beginning of wisdom." I felt that. I felt it like a thickness in the air. What kept me trying to resist temptations, at those times when I thought I recognized them, was the fear of God, the fear of his punishment, the fear of misfortunes he might unleash.

Later there came a time when I decided that God was not watching as closely as I had feared. Considering the terrible villainies he had let various terrible people get away with over the centuries, and hearing something about great evils still going on, I thought God was probably uninterested in anything as trivial as my doings. Good or bad, they must seem insignificant to him as he surveys the whole panorama of the universe, I thought. Eventually I wondered whether in fact he might be completely uninvolved with all human-

3

ity. He might even be nonexistent. Could he perhaps be safely ignored? With some hope I set about excluding him from my thoughts, my feelings, and my choices—mind, heart, and will.

Still later came a time when I was angry at God. Somehow I was unable to ignore him and be rid of him. The question "But suppose it is all true?" kept intruding into my consciousness, whether I was thinking about the world, looking for "truth," wrestling with decisions, or searching for emotional satisfaction and personal fulfillment. It was an intrusion I deeply resented. Why should I have to make an effort to doubt? It was no effort to doubt the existence of the Abominable Snowman, or flying saucers, or Santa Claus. What was so special about "God"? Or let him exist if he wanted to exist, like possible intelligent spiders on a planet of some far-off star, but why should I have to think about either him or them? Why should I even have to think about the issue of thinking about him? Privacy was impossible if there was some God watching all my actions and even reading all my thoughts. Bitterly I desired nothing more than to be left alone, even if that should leave me in misery. The mere fact of God's existence appeared to me to be an intrusion into my freedom, and even into my self.

Such shifts in attitude toward God are not unusual. Quite a few well-known authors have chronicled their changes of view, and you may have read some of those spiritual odysseys. What's more, looking around the world and back through history we find the variety of attitudes toward God greatly multiplied. People have had a bewildering variety of concepts of God, and concepts influence attitudes.

Those who think of God as so tolerant, or alien, or impersonal, or preoccupied that he takes no interest in us, tend, naturally, to take no interest in him. Those who believe he is cruel, ready to afflict people with all kinds of disasters like crop failures, loathsome diseases, and general bad luck, if he is not appeased with whatever he demands—anything from a simple rain dance to a human sacrifice —naturally tend to be fearful and subservient toward him, or toward those who appear to be his authorized agents. The most casual study of comparative religion turns up examples of practices ranging from the silly to the unspeakably depraved, judged by our standards, all seriously supported by some theory about God.

Some have concluded from this variety that there can be no certainty of any kind about God. Some are therefore quick to quash any discussion aimed at exploring for truth about God and what his proclamations about humanity might imply. "Well, you may feel that way, but I feel differently," they may say. "You have your concept of God and I have mine, and everyone really has a right to his own concept."

This is very hard to rebut because it is so true. But it does have a serious weakness in that it overlooks one very important possibility: God might be real.

Some Differences between an Unreal God and a Real God

If God is not real—if there is nothing above the universe to talk about, no reality corresponding to this name "God" which we hear from time to time—then one person's concept is indeed as good as any other person's. It might be better to say that one person's concept is as idiotic as any other person's in such circumstances. If God is a figment of human imagination, then certainly my figment is no better than your figment. This is the view of the candid atheist, but it must be noted that his zero-God concept is only one more concept, with no logical ground for preference above the other concepts of God. The atheist is really as much a believer as Believers.

There is also a school of thought which declines to believe, and makes a virtue of not knowing. Here can be found a variety of outlooks, some admirable and some not so admirable. Some in this category have simply not lived long enough to feel that they have heard all they should hear before trying to settle so great a question, and in a very candid humility they say they do not know whether God is real or not. No one can find fault with such agnostics, but they are not the ones who will avoid discussion. Rather they are likely to be among the most interested in hearing anyone who seems to have something to offer that might help with the fundamental questions about God and man, life and death, origin, destiny, and meaning.

Others among the agnostics, however, deliberately turned their backs on the search for knowledge or experience which might end their not-knowing. They speak patronizingly of all who have any belief, approving the idea of having "faith in a higher power" though they themselves do not believe. Their view implies that indulging in the practice of believing in something above yourself can be healthy and socially useful, even if it is a delusion. They certainly do not see more validity in one concept of God than in another, as long as they all seem harmless, but they do seem to give you more approval if you show consistency or intensity in the faith with which you remain

6

committed to your chosen delusion. They seem to regard this as helping psychological "adjustment." Switching delusions is tolerated, intellectually and socially, but only "sincere" delusion-switching is admired. Cynical switching—to sell insurance, or advance social status, or gain political advantage—is frowned on. So is forcing an argument with "believers." The highest-ranking in their catalogue of virtues is tolerance.

If that school's view of reality were well-founded, we would be much like a group of children among whom the more sophisticated don't believe Santa Claus is real but do enjoy encouraging belief among the younger ones, agreeing that pretending makes Christmas more fun for all. In those circumstances it doesn't matter if some think the elves should be included in the pretending, as Santa's helpers. It doesn't matter if some include Mrs. Claus in the story, or if some have added a red-nosed intruder to the traditional eight reindeer, particularly since the eight are themselves relatively recent additions to an older version of how Santa Claus travels back and forth delivering goodies.

But if Santa Claus were real, things would be quite different. The way in which request letters were addressed might suddenly matter. Portraits on greeting cards might have to be adjusted. More pillows, or fewer, might be needed under the costumes of any imitators, and the costumes might need to be changed completely.

When science-fiction writers and weavers of fantasy wrote about life on Mars before our satellites started to land there and send back photographs and soil analyses and information on the atmosphere and the temperature, all kinds of native Martian civilizations could be imagined. If you read Ray Bradbury you got one impression. Heinlein's *Stranger in a Strange Land* gave another. The saga of John Carter and Thuvia by Edgar Rice Burroughs postulated still another view of Mars. But now Mars has emerged from the unknowable to the unknown, and from the unknown to the partially known, and all stories about it from now on will be affected. As long as it was unknowable, almost any speculation was credible. That is the situation now with flying saucers. And if God is unknowable, who can discredit any concept about him?

7

Now suppose for a moment that one of those flying saucers which are occasionally reported as visiting our planet were to land on the White House lawn some Thanksgiving morning and Santa Claus should step out. He could easily demonstrate his indisputable claim over all the impostors in the department-store parades, and he could tell us what he really called his reindeer, if he used any, before he moved on to advanced transportation technology. Then we might know whether the story of Rudolph was travesty or insight.

If that should happen, and Santa Claus were seen beyond question to be real, then someone would have been closer to the truth and someone else farther from it. Some might be nearly right about Santa, or all might be quite wrong. Concepts would stand or fall after being measured against the reality.

Advance and be Recognized!

For better or for worse, Santa hasn't stepped out of a flying saucer onto the White House lawn yet. And if he had, it might not be a flying saucer he stepped out of. And if it were a flying saucer which landed, it might not be Santa who would step out. In fact, saucers, and what may or may not step out of them, are the object of almost as much curious uncertainty as God.

For quite a few years now there have been recurring reports of what have come to be called "Unidentified Flying Objects" in the sky, and on the ground as well. Some who claim to have been eyewitnesses say the UFOs look like saucers in flight. Others have variously described them as "cigar-shaped," "shaped like a football and pitted like coral rock," "white and egg-shaped," "brilliant red and roundish," "a giant wing two hundred feet long with pulsating lights at each end," "elliptical with a tail on the bottom," and on and on. Those who claim to have been taken for rides on them sometimes throw in a great deal more detail. If each different vision had produced a "church" of believers, the UFO enthusiasts would need an ecumenical movement by now. But they have not moved in the direction of defining orthodoxy and holding heresy trials yet. Maybe if they get larger and stronger, perhaps officially adopted and recognized by a president of the United States, such splits might begin to appear. For the moment they subordinate their differences to the uniting factor of their insistence that our planet has been visited by a civilization transcending ours.

This they have in common with people who believe in the Incarnation, actually, though there is a difference between thinking that superior beings have come in spaceships and thinking that the Supreme Being has come in the form of a man. The common element of belief is that there is something transcending humanity. But when we try to get down to details, we find that the ideas reported about God vary as widely as those about UFOs. God is thought of as the Cosmic Killjoy, the Absent-Minded Universe-Starter, the Genial Man Upstairs, the Great Top-Sergeant-in-the-Sky, the Obsolete

9

Tribal Mascot, the Out-of-Date Idealist, and more. If we reach into the corners of our past we find him thought of also as the Sadistic Virgin-Devourer, the Periodic Sun-Stealer, the Angry Volcano-Spirit, the Capricious Weather-Maker—and it is hard to say which set of ideas, ancient or modern, is more false or foolish in an ultimate sense. At any rate, both lists could be prolonged until you find the game of research and phrasemaking no longer amusing. The uncertainty and the controversy persist because God has this in common with Santa and the saucers: none of them has landed on the White House lawn, or any other "important" place. I suspect someone must have already said that God is not dead, he is just unidentified.

This is where Santa Claus, saucers, and God all come together in the underlying assumptions implicit in today's popular thought. They all fall into the category of things not proved by the standards of proof that we generally seem to demand. There is, however, evidence of sloppy thinking and double standards in these matters. There is unequal treatment in our minds, around our dinner tables, in our politics, and throughout our social patterns. Say something provocative about visitors from outer space at a dinner party and you may be thought witty and clever. Say something provocative about God in the same setting and you will be thought gauche or rude. You may even panic the hostess. Try a similar comment about Santa Claus and you will be looked at strangely. There may be titters of embarrassment. No one will be sure whether to laugh or to think you were drinking too much before dinner. Persist and you may be recommended to a psychiatrist. But if you don't take Santa seriously, anything you say will be acceptable. It is perfectly all right to enjoy Santa, but not to believe. Believing in flying saucers is regarded as only mildly eccentric, however, and open-mindedness is fully accepted. Open-mindedness about the reality of Santa Claus could get you committed to an institution.

God is the most delicate subject of the three. If you are going into presidential politics, it is easy to figure out what you should answer a reporter who asks about your belief in Santa Claus or UFOs, but a similar question about God is trickier. Santa you pass off with a smile as a joke. You and the reporter are insiders together, going along with a gag for the children's sake. Deceiving children is not generally admired, but we make an exception. On UFOs you put on a most serious expression and deprecate the whole thing, saying "there is no evidence to prove . . ." and you express confidence that the Air Force studies and the scientific establishment will take care of the whole thing. You can easily see, however, that you must not give that kind of answer about Santa Claus, or about God. Think how it would sound if you should speak of them saying "there is no evidence to prove. . . ." Believing in God has been expected of presidents, however. A candidate who treated belief in God as a joke would be in trouble. But it is also regarded as risky to make a point of taking belief in God seriously in politics or in business or in a university. There are even some religious denominations where taking belief in God seriously might not do your career much good. For politicains belief is supposed to be there, but in the background, under control, not dominant. In most segments of our society, in fact, a form of belief in God is expected, but it is regarded as foolish to let this interfere with a "practical" view of life, and that means a view which leaves God out.

So a typical well-adjusted modern is supposed to look at Santa Claus, flying saucers, and God—all not proved—and ridicule one, leave one to science, and ignore the third. The ridicule should be gentle, the deference to science should be skeptical, and the ignoring should be tolerant. All this would change if there were a landing in an Important Place. Such a landing is the kind of thing we would like to have any and all higher powers do, so that we could apply the scientific method to them, starting with observation and investigation. We stand prepared to pass judgment, with our mental tools and weapons at the ready. We're all set to give God or Santa or visitors from another world the same intellectual courtesies we would offer a new subatomic particle or a new species of sea creature from a mile down in the ocean. "Advance and be recognized!"

It's almost funny, like children playing with a bomb. We don't know whether we could even survive the presence on our earth of

11

a being from a distant unknown world, to say nothing of the Creator of all worlds. And if God, or some super-stranger, should thoughtfully shield himself so as to be able to come and visit without damaging us, how would we react to such a "soft landing"? Would we miss it altogether? Or might we perhaps mock and crucify him?

How to Serve Man

Before any judgment is passed on those who might miss or mock or martyr a "soft landing" by a super-being, consider the message of an imaginative science fiction author who has written of a day when visitors from another world suddenly landed their flying saucers at a great many Important Places on earth—not only the White House lawn but also Red Square, Hyde Park, the Boston Common, and every other location that really counts.

The visitors came out making signs of peace and friendship, and talking our languages. They said they had been watching the human race for centuries and had developed a great liking and admiration for us as we wrestled with our difficulties and advanced our levels of understanding and capability. In fact the book which came closest in their culture to being the equivalent of our Bible, they said, was a volume entitled *How to Serve Man*. This, they explained, was what they lived for, and what they had traveled across the galaxy for.

Their actions fit right in with their words. They promptly showed humanity scientific and economic secrets that wiped out all poverty and disease. The threat of starvation vanished from the earth, and the billions of gaunt bodies rounded quickly into robust specimens of perfect health. Energy became plentiful and cheap. Luxuries abounded. Crime and war became pointless. Even politicians turned honest.

To make a story out of the situation, of course, the writer had to introduce some dramatic tension. These fantastically superior beings were fantastically careless, or the technology which brought them across the reaches of space somehow did not produce an adequate burglar alarm system for their ships. So two suspicious humans, who thought the whole thing a great deal too good to be true, succeeded in getting on one of the space ships for more than the guided tour.

Their worst fears were justified. They crept through the vessel until they found a copy of the volume which the aliens had called their sacred book. When they looked inside it they realized to their horror the double meaning of the title. *How to Serve Man* was a cookbook.

Those super-beings were not nice. Fortunately they were not real either. But how about other super-beings, if any? Are any real? If so, are they nice? Would they regard us as cattle, or ants? How about Santa Claus? Have we all been undergoing some subtle brainwashing for centuries, victims of hypnotic suggestion to condition us into an attitude of friendliness toward white-bearded fat men in red suits so that when the invasion comes we will not put up any resistance? If Santa Claus is breeding an elf army in secret Arctic caverns, I want to know about it. The same goes for flying saucers that might be setting up a secret base in the distant recesses of the Amazon jungles. Is it really safe to take a "you can't be serious!" attitude toward Santa Claus? Are our scientists too prejudiced and fearful for their reputations to do an honest job of warning us about flying saucers? Are their investigative techniques adequate?

And how about God? Even if he is not dead, can he be trusted? What does he really want from us? What does he want to do with us, or to us? Does he want to consume our souls, somehow, as the space visitors in the story wanted to consume our flesh? After all, we have heard fearful tales about how the devil's offers of wealth and power should be shunned because the deal will cost us our souls. Is God really any better than the devil in this respect, if there is any devil? What does God want with our souls?

The most important question about God is not whether he is real. I hope you see that. Even if the uncertainty about his reality could be indisputably settled, there still remains the far more vital question of what he is like and how that will affect us. The same goes for Santa and visitors from outer space. If God is real, is he good? Is he friendly? Is he safe? Are his goals and aspirations compatible in any sense with ours? Is God a potential ally or a threat as we struggle with the problems of our race and of our personalities? Is he for us or against us? Should we, in our own best interests, trust him or resist him?

And how can we find out?

Getting Serious about UFOs, and "The Hidden God"

Looking at super-beings from a nonfictional point of view, we find the best-informed scientists saying now that there may well be whole civilizations of them in existence. There are a great many galaxies in the universe according to our observations, and a great many stars in each galaxy. Many of those stars could well have systems of planets, just as our sun has. Judging from what we can deduce about the stars we see in our telescopes, some highly reputable scientists believe that there could be as many as two hundred million earthlike planets on which there could be intelligent life as we might recognize it, and that figure is for this galaxy alone.

In addition to these possibilities, we must consider the chance of intelligent life in forms we would find completely unlike ourselves. Nothing remotely approaching human life could exist on a small hot airless planet such as we believe Mercury to be, or on a huge poisonous planet such as we believe Jupiter to be, but that does not mean that intelligence could not thrive in those places in some completely alien form. The same goes for other planets of other stars in our galaxy, and in the other galaxies.

But even if we limit our consideration to planets where flesh and blood beings like ourselves could flourish, we are talking about hundreds of millions of possible civilizations, according to the best current guesses of our most learned men and women. Some of those possible races of beings out there might be in states of development which we would call primitive. Others might be much more advanced. It is highly unlikely that any particular life form would be at precisely the level of technological achievement where we happen to be right now, and a small difference in level of achievement could have a very large effect. After all, only a generation ago most people thought of space travel as ridiculous. Nobody took Flash Gordon seriously, and very few even took Goddard and Von Braun seriously. Go back just a little farther, only a century or two, and anyone talking seriously about being visited by life forms from other worlds

15

would have run the serious risk of being burned as a heretic or a witch. We are beyond that particular kind of irrational response now, but we are not yet able to achieve space travel, or even to detect interstellar flight in our part of the universe with any certainty. This is a very narrow band in the history of development.

If we assume that the age of our planet is several billion years, and if we represent that by the tallest building on earth, then the longest guess about the time humanity has been on the planet would be equivalent to the thickness of a couple of telephone books placed on the top of the skyscraper. On that same scale, the length of time we call historic, with written records of our race's history, would be equivalent to the thickness of a postage stamp on the phone books on top of the building. The time we call "modern," this moment of open-mindedness about flying saucers, would be less than the thickness of the glue on the stamp on the phone books on the skyscraper.

What we would probably find if we could look in on other races, then—if there are any—would be that they are either far behind us or far ahead of us, rather than sharing our particular combination of ability and inability. They might have discovered steam power when we were building pyramids, for example. That would make them almost incredibly close to our own exact stage of development. But in that situation they might well have discovered atomic power and rockets just a hundred years after steam, as we did. Who can imagine what they might have discovered in the several thousand years since that time? Think what our science might be able to achieve a few thousand years from now if we solve the problems that threaten our survival today. It's not hard to believe that we might find a way to go star-hopping by then, popping in on planets that might support life, and possibly meeting a race of beings just in the quaint stage of first flights to their moon and landing unmanned probes on their neighboring planets.

We might then decide to test their science by letting them catch a glimpse of some of our ships occasionally. We could laugh tolerantly as they launched jet planes to try to investigate our star-cruisers, and we could neutralize their electronic sensing devices just to observe how they behave when bewildered. With our superiority

16

it would certainly be our decision, not theirs, as to whether they would learn anything about us or get to see us. We could reveal ourselves or remain hidden.

Obviously so can God, if God is real. This is the significance of the phrase made famous by Karl Barth, the late Swiss theologian, when he spoke of "the hidden God." On our own, we are not in a position to determine either the reality of God or his character. Clearly it has always been his decision as to whether or not we could know anything about him. Clearly he is in a position to send messages or to send none, and to prescribe just how those messages, if any, can be received and understood.

If God is real, we are at his mercy.

Much to Hope from the Flowers

We have now accumulated three rather significant and difficult questions. First, is God actually real or unreal? Second, if he is real, what is he like? And finally, how can we possibly find answers to the first two questions since a real God could so easily remain hidden?

It is difficult to regard it as a complete coincidence that the heart of the message of the Bible—the world's best-known book—is a set of answers to precisely these questions. It would certainly be wonderfully convenient, in view of the problems involved in trying on our own to go about finding definitive and trustworthy answers to those three questions, if the answers were in fact easily available. It would be even more pleasant if the available answers were pleasant and reassuring, and if we could be certain they were the right answers. Basically the message of the Bible is that God is real, that his nature is love, and that he has gone to considerable trouble to become known to us, trying to reveal himself in ways designed to win our trust. It is not surprising that this proclamation is referred to again and again in that book as the "good news." But can we accept that biblical proclamation as reliable? What clues do we have, and what do they indicate?

Sherlock Holmes, the great detective story hero who is supposed to have been fictional but in whom quite a few adults like to say they believe, has some thoughts to offer on this subject. There is a point in one story where we find the master standing by a window, deep in thought, looking intently at a rose. Since Holmes is the embodiment of cool intellect and logical deduction, his friend Dr. Watson comes over to see if he has discovered some new clue to the mystery they are pursuing. But Holmes says his thoughts were not on the case at that moment. He was thinking, he says, about what man can deduce from the flowers.

Human beings need air to breathe, water to drink, food for nourishment, the sun for energy, and all the other things that sustain physical life, Holmes points out to Watson. But beauty, he says, is not strictly necessary. Beauty is extra, and with beauty comes much

18

joy and pleasure for us. Therefore, Holmes deduces, the intelligence behind the universe, which he calls Providence, must be benevolent. In Holmes's words, "Man has much to hope from the flowers."

The universe is indeed so full of beauty that only a complete grouch can fail to be moved by the flowers, stars, waterfalls, redwood trees, dolphins, sunsets, the laughter of children, and all the other created loveliness around us. We know from some of the more gruesome aberrations of contemporary history that human beings can survive for astonishing lengths of time deprived of these joyful and beautiful experiences. The prison camps and torture chambers of a variety of governments, totalitarian and nominally otherwise, have shown how barren and harsh an environment can be in which humans can still survive and even perpetuate the species. An unpleasant contribution to this insight is made by the slums in any large city. Humanity has contrived, sometimes by design and sometimes by neglect, to produce some incredibly bad conditions in which people have been forced to live. The natural environment is happily not that harsh. Our universe is not modeled after the minimum. The rich profusion of beauty is one of the plain facts that philosophers must face along with the less pleasant data.

If the universe is created, this is an important indication of the character and motives of the Creator. And if there is a real God worthy of the name, the universe must be created. No being simply coexisting in the universe with us, a fellow entity, could rightly be thought of as God. A fellow entity lording it over us, benignly or otherwise, could be a powerful influence, like a technological man among primitives, but that is not what we are looking for when we ask if there is anybody "Up There." A real God must be regarded rather as the provident creative intelligence from which, or from whom, we and all other entities both "animate" and "inanimate" have come. If there is such a being, then his action in creating our environment does indeed give some valuable and encouraging clues. From seeing his work as artist and engineer, and the presence of the extras like beauty, we can begin to know something about him. A creator who makes flowers can't be all bad.

19

Dr. No and Dr. Yes;
More Clues from Prehistory

Speaking of flowers, it was a garden full of beautiful fruits and flowers in which man is reported to have first found himself. For the moment, let us pass the question of whether the report is factual or symbolic. Whether it is an account of actual events or some allegory emerging out of ancient wisdom, it carries some interesting clues. At its most obvious level, it certainly tells us at least that we had a pleasant start here. God shouldn't have done things that way if he was trying to hide or to terrify. The Garden of Eden was certainly not a minimum beginning.

We all give ourselves away when we open our mouths, or when we do anything. Contemporary best-sellers have told us that even when we stand or sit still the way we arrange our bodies communicates our character nonverbally. By these channels of information God was certainly giving away some important data about his personality when he put Adam and Eve in a paradise. Before that, who would have guessed that God would even want to be bothered making an Other of any kind? Why should he share the quality of Being? Before humanity was given such an idyllic environment for launching, there might even have been doubts in our minds about accepting existence, if we could have been given the choice in some preliminary form of consciousness. "What's it going to be like?"

In the first book of Ian Fleming's famous series about secret agent James Bond, alias 007, we read of a luxurious private world created by a brilliant and powerful person named Dr. No. Bond was not invited into this private world. When he arrived, he was not made welcome. In fact his presence was violently resented. Dr. No captured Bond and set out to take his life, putting him into a specially designed torture maze. The crowning cruelty for Bond was that he was deprived of the company of any beautiful women, a comfort he was accustomed to. Dr. No did his worst to Bond, reserving the best of his world for himself. Cruelty gave him pleasure.

In the first book of the Bible we have an account of a situation so diametrically opposed that one wonders whether Ian Fleming was consciously arranging the contrast. We read in Genesis of a luxurious world created by a brilliant and powerful being whom we might call Dr. Yes. Adam and Eve were invited into existence in this world, and beyond mere existence, into authority over it and friendship with the Creator. Their presence was definitely and enthusiastically enjoyed. Dr. Yes gave them both life and freedom, placing them in the specially designed pleasure garden. The crowning joy for Adam was that he was not left alone, but was completed and delighted by the partnership of a beautiful woman, a comfort beyond anything he had been able to find or imagine as he had encountered the other creatures. Dr. Yes did his best for Adam and Eve, and shared even something of his own nature with them. That kind of giving gave him pleasure.

In the torture maze there was every kind of pain that could make a person suffer. In the Garden of Eden there was every tree that was pleasant to the sight and good for food. In the torture maze there was only one way to survive. In the Garden of Eden there was only one way to get in trouble. In the torture maze, when Bond found the way out, Dr. No angrily tried again to destroy him. In the Garden of Eden, when Adam and Eve fell into the only trap, God immediately launched a great rescue and rehabilitation operation.

There are objections that the rescue is taking too long, causing many to doubt God's reality or goodness, or both. But how long is too long? What is the true measure of time? There are strong hints in the Bible that time itself is part of the problem, part of the situation requiring the rescue operation or part of the rescue technique. It is suggested that time had a beginning and will have an end, and that before the beginning and after the end there is ("was" and "will be" seem less to the point) some other mode of experiencing. We are so steeped in time that we can hardly imagine any other mode of experiencing, but we cannot deny that such a mode is possible, and that the concept of eternity tries to suggest it. So time may, in the end, turn out not to have been a very real commodity at all. This would certainly take the sting out of the objection that the rescue is taking "too long." The complaints could vanish re-

21

troactively. For the moment this is speculation, to be sure, but it is speculation suggested by some highly intriguing details in the biblical view of history.

In any case, we are told that we are now living, in time, through the rescue operation. What's more, we are assured that it will have an unimaginably happy ending, which will really be more of a beginning.

Section II

A Section Designed to Expose Some
Weaknesses in the Ways We Usually
Look for Answers, and to Let You
Feel Free with No Guilt about Having
Some Longings and Being Interested
in Pleasure as Well as in Truth

Do Parallel Lines Meet?

There have been a few unsubstantiated assertions sprinkled through the last several pages, and there will be more coming up. There is also the matter of the Bible, introduced and quoted without any foundation having been laid for its reliability, if any. This is not the way a search for truth ordinarily proceeds in our experience.

But we must remember that in trying to learn about God, who could so easily hide, we are in an entirely different ball game. We cannot play by our ordinary rules, and must try to discover as we go along what the new rules are. I realize that a logically inclined person trained in the scientific method may boggle at some of this, but to such a person who is sincere in searching for truth let me address three suggestions.

First, observe that truth is not the only goal of the human personality, and that the mind is not the whole person. We have as a race been living through several centuries in which the rational powers of humanity have been receiving so much attention and honor that the rest has been relatively neglected. Some sense of this imbalance is developing in our time, and there is a new surge of interest in getting in touch with our bodies and our feelings. Many are astounded to find that we can control, with practice, various physical functions which had been thought beyond our reach. There are hints that we might have other latent powers, forgotten by a long stretch of too much reliance on reason. And we have seen that all the powers of the reason are threatened when a person loses contact with the inner desires and emotions.

We are in a position something like that of a young boy who decides to develop a strong body, and who then launches into a ten-year program of lifting weights with his right hand while lying on his back. He may get a fantastically strong right arm and shoulder, but the rest of the body will remain weak, and some parts could atrophy.

This brings me to the second suggestion. Note that our achievement of the other things we search for in addition to truth—such as love, freedom, pleasure, peace—is not automatically assisted when our minds make advances in the rational search for truth. The history of the last two generations offers ample proof of that. The advances of technology have not always and necessarily enhanced our overall quality of life. New discoveries have brought new dangers as we have found the development of interpersonal relations inadequate to guarantee that we will use what we know in our own best interests. We find ourselves on the threshhold of destroying our own species, and all the others as well, both directly through nuclear war and indirectly through the polluting side effects of our industry.

A third suggestion to those who are steeped in the rational method of search, and to admirers of its undeniable achievements, is that they consider the fact that even at its purest and best rationalism has some serious inherent weaknesses. "Proof before belief!" is a slogan with a solid and sensible sound, but it has a key flaw. For even in the rational method all proof rests on foundations that must simply be accepted. This is not always clearly recognized by the person without scientific training, to whom the word "proof" has a comforting ring. But let me remind you of the proofs in plane geometry, since that is where most of us have encountered at least some introduction to the idea of proof. Statements in any proof must be backed up with reasons, and the only acceptable reasons in proving a theorem are axioms, postulates, and previously proved theorems. Those previously proved theorems were themselves proved on the basis of axioms, postulates, and theorems proved still earlier, and so going backward we see that the entire structure rests ultimately on nothing but axioms and postulates, which are taken on faith—simply accepted. All proof rests on foundations of faith. Some philosophers of science have tried to give more validity to certain sets of assumptions over others by saying that the most conservative and limited assumptions needed to explain something are truer and more to be accepted, requiring less faith, than fancy and complicated assumptions. But even this preference for minimal assumptions is itself an assumption, either pure arbitrary preference or an exercise of faith, implying that the Creator would prefer the "Bauhaus" style to "Art Nouveau."

26

Do Parallel Lines Meet?

Faith in some set of accepted basics is fundamental to all kinds of proof, and there is no way around that primary act of acceptance. If experiment later clashes with a result predicted by derivation from proved propositions, then the underlying axioms are reexamined and jettisoned, to be replaced with a new set, again taken on faith, so that another system of proof can be constructed that will not clash with observed results. And this whole system rests also on faith in our capacity to observe results reliably.

So it happened that Einstein's work led to the general consensus that our faith in Euclid's axioms of geometry had been misplaced. We had thought it obvious for a couple of thousand years, for example, that parallel lines would never meet, no matter how far extended. Since Einstein, however, scientists have placed their faith in a contrary view. They now believe that space is curved, and that therefore parallel lines always meet if you extend them far enough.

And next year?

The Limits of Reason

With science so plainly ephemeral, and resting on changing sets of assumptions, we have to think again about just what it is we want when we say we want proof. What we really mean, since we are the kind of beings we are, is that we want certainty. We want confidence, and we want assurances that our confidence is not misplaced. We want to know. We want to be sure, in the gut as well as in the mind. And "scientific proof" can no longer provide such assurances and certainty.

The finest scientists have been the first to admit this and to abandon the old pretensions of science in this regard. The almost superstitious faith in science of many nonscientists has lingered longer, but in our time it has fortunately lost the grip it had when this century began. The scientists have gradually learned to live with the unsettling idea that the most carefully and rigorously proved structures of thought rest on the very unsettled foundations of assumptions. They have learned to speak of science as descriptive and functional rather than as explanatory and true.

This humility has been learned rather slowly, and not without pain. There have been a number of periods in human history when the consensus was that mankind had fully, or at least very nearly, rounded out the complete sum of all knowledge and understanding. But new questions and new evidence and new anomalies have always come along to challenge the most confidently held theories, and new theories have again and again been needed to replace the most enduring structures of thought.

Remember the time when the ancients had it all settled, with the earth surrounded by a river called Ocean, and the whole thing resting on the shoulders of a giant, Atlas, since it obviously couldn't be hanging on nothing? Quite a number of years later, someone—probably an unusually difficult teenager—wondered out loud what Atlas was standing on. Finally, after some fooling around with theories about elephants and giant turtles, the problem of ultimate

28

foundations—the difficulty of really getting to the bottom of things —was recognized, and the old approach to the support of the earth was abandoned.

Those old cosmologies which were current so long ago seem silly to us now. But how much of our scientific and other systematic thought will seem silly only a hundred years from now, to say nothing of a thousand years from now? Just a few years ago the idea that South America had once fitted into Africa was smiled at as the unsophisticated fantasy of a child getting a first look at a world map and jumping to ridiculous conclusions. But now most students of geology believe that's just the way it once was.

As recently as about a hundred years ago a young man named Max Planck was advised by his professors not to pursue physics as a career since there was nothing important left to discover. But Planck persisted, working on some mysteries most scientists thought were trivial, and in 1900 he announced a revolutionary concept of energy bundles he called "quanta." That ushered in the whole new era which is now called "modern" physics as opposed to "classical" physics. But what will "modern" physics be called after the next breakthrough?

It has not been too long since mathematicians stopped asserting that a straight line is always the shortest distance between two points, but now we have non-Euclidean geometries that say the shortest distance between two points is a curve. Looking a bit farther back at one of the founders of rationalism, Descartes, we see that what was once the basis of his philosophy has become the caption of a *New Yorker* cartoon. Two astonished men in lab smocks are shown bending over the printout tape from a giant computer and seeing the now-famous Latin words: *Cogito, ergo sum*—"I think, therefore I am."

The era in which thought was considered man's highest power, and reason was considered the beginning and the end of everything, is passing. If reason does not tell us that it cannot work alone, it has not done its most important job. This is sinking in, and few are so foolish any longer as to try to accomplish anything within the bounds of reason alone. Pure mind is not necessarily the original state of all things or the ideal state. Gradually we are all beginning to get the full significance of the Danish philosopher Kierkegaard's great saying that the function of reason is to show us the limits of reason.

The Leap of Faith

So it turns out that using reason as a starting point and trying to "get to the bottom of things" is misusing reason. The bottom isn't something you get to; it's something you start at. We must choose our foundations, just as the scientists must. Kierkegaard summed it up in another famous phrase, saying we all must take a "leap of faith." Faith chooses the foundations on which reason can build.

But taking a leap of faith when the course of your whole life is at stake can be rather a dizzying prospect, and more disturbing when the alternatives are actively and noisily competing. The difficulties of decision make some hesitant to the point of saying they refuse to leap. Others seem astonishingly ready to leap in the most surprising directions, ready to put their faith in what seems like sheer nonsense to the rest of us.

For all of us, of whatever temperament, for the most cautious as well as for the most credulous, the choice is as important as the selection of a foundation in building a house, and for the same reasons. We build our lives on our most fundamental choice. Our lives will be happy, satisfying to us and useful to others, or they will be frustrating and purposeless, depending on that choice. In the end it determines whether we live or die.

Some choose to put their faith in themselves. This is the leap of those who claim they are not leaping. It is also a choice made consciously and proudly by others, trying to be their own foundations. In spite of all the limitations of human brain and strength, senses and instruments, they decide to believe only what can be proved to them, starting from what they themselves can observe and calculate. A somewhat plaintive statement of this case is occasionally heard in the phrase "I may not be much, but I'm all I've got." Even if all humanity says this in chorus, making a statement of faith in the race, the same limitations prevail.

A refinement of this position is to try to weed out the more obviously confused and venal specimens of humanity and to trust in science, regarding it as the product of humanity's intellectual elite.

Some still do this, in spite of all the disagreements among various schools of scientific thought, in spite of all the unexplained phenomena science does not pretend to understand, in spite of all the elements of life over which science cannot exercise any control at all, and in spite of the certainty that tomorrow's science will pass the very harshest judgment on today's science by exposing its oversights and replacing it bit by bit with a new model, which will itself be outdated and replaced in the next age.

Some who have been disillusioned with the shifting sands of science, or chilled by its impersonal sterility, choose instead to put their ultimate confidence in some philosophical, political, or moral system. They are perhaps both shocked and frightened that a branch of what calls itself the science of the soul, psychology, has in our time come up with a program for going "beyond freedom and dignity." They search for a movement, devised and administered by some great leader or group of leaders, grappling with the great human problems of the times in terms of values. They hope that somehow the limitations and weaknesses of such persons, a kind of spiritual elite, will be less dangerous flaws in the foundations of their lives than their own limitations or the shortcomings of science.

But all these foundations have at least some acknowledged weaknesses. All involve people. People do the formulating, or the interpreting, or the administering, or all three, and all those people at some time or another have to share in the great confession of our race: "We're only human!" The implications are unavoidable. If it is true that "we're all we've got," with nobody "Up There," then such a reliance on our best might be the wisest course. It might also be the best course if we realized that there were more powerful and reliable beings "Up There" in whom we might place our faith, but realized at the same time that they were hostile or indifferent to our needs and aspirations.

Santa Claus might be the perfect alternative, but we've pretty much decided that he isn't real. It's rather a shame, because we seem pretty much convinced that he's friendly. Trusting some super-race that might be visiting in the flying saucers seems like a long shot. Most writers dealing with this possibility do not think it likely that such aliens will be congenial or even compatible with humans. In any case it's an alternative we can do nothing about since we have to wait, it would seem, either for them to arrive or for our technology to enable us to put salt on their tails. There are a few who choose to believe that they have arrived and have delivered advice that should be followed. That is another option. But it quickly leads us to ask: "Is there anybody *else* up there?"

Faith and/or Certainty

Consider now the possibility of finding a foundation with no limitations at all. That's what it would be like to found your life and thought on God, if God is real and if he is good for us. Consider what it might be like to find the source and ground of all being, the force behind or above or at the bottom of the whole universe, men and systems included. The potential of what we as persons, including our minds, might be able to build on such a foundation is hardly imaginable. In fact it may well be completely beyond the capacities of our imaginations in their present state.

There are two possible objections to standing on even this perfect foundation, however, or maybe they are two facets of the same objection. First, the very existence of such a God, it might be feared, could stunt our growth, leaving us with a destiny of being nothing more than happy pets, and that seems to us incompatible with our nature even if we were unconscious of any frustration or inferiority feelings. We have a quality, sometimes called pride or ambition or racial consciousness, which tells us that settling for any such domesticated bliss would be cheating ourselves somehow. Quite a few serious writers imply that we should struggle against any "god" who would in any way limit our greatness, if there is a god, even if the struggle were completely hopeless. Better to die free than to live enslaved.

This is a deeply rooted human feeling, and I do not find that it is in any way wrong or offensive to God. Some theories about God have objected to this attitude, but when we get to a closer examination of what first went wrong between God and humanity I think it will become clear that human arrogance was not the problem.

The second objection to trusting even a perfect God is related to the first. Some fear that starting with faith of any kind, in any foundation, might force us to abandon our yearning for real total certainty. Our judgment might be swallowed up and lost, just as our identity or our destiny might. But this objection, like the other, will vanish, I believe, when we take a good look at what God really

suggests when he invites us to put our faith in him as the ultimate
and perfect foundation.

He does not ask us to stop searching for knowledge through the
use of reason, for one thing. But he does ask us to recognize that he
cannot be classed with rocks and vitamins, flora and fauna, to be
manipulated and studied at our pleasure, or dissected through ways
and means of our choice. He cannot be known that way, and he
wants us to see and accept that fact.

This should not surprise us, or violate anything we hold dear,
since we should be able to see clearly that a different method of
learning is needed even when we try to know our fellow human
beings. We need an "I-Thou" relationship rather than an "I-It"
attitude, to use Martin Buber's famous terms. There are things we
can classify as objects, and treat and investigate as objects. We call
any such thing "it." But some degree of mutual consent and cooperation must be developed before we can know each other. We must
address persons; we cannot know them by treating them as objects.
Relating to persons as economic objects, political objects, sex objects, or intellectual objects, will always introduce distortions.

It is even more important to realize that treating God as an object
will not work. We must address him. If we want to know our
Creator, who is the ground of all being, it will certainly not be
through the ordinary methods of science, appropriate in dealing
with objects, that we must proceed. We are not in a position to
dictate terms. God's consent and cooperation are needed if we want
to know him, even more than the consent and cooperation of fellow
humans we want to know.

What God tells us about how to find him is this: We must trust
him if we are to know him. That is a reversal of the usual order of
"I-It" investigation, but it has precedent in human interpersonal
relationships. God does not, however, ask us to put our faith blindly
in him and then shout loudly that we see. He asks, rather, that we
come to him and let the experience of knowing him open our eyes.
Then, he promises, we will be able to see him and all things as they
really are, including ourselves. We must know him personally before
we can know him rationally.

God does not ask us to abandon reason. He is the one who made our inquiring minds. He asks that we let him reconcile the conflict between faith and inquiry, the conflict which the tyranny of reason has stirred up. God offers to bring us to the place where we can experience the union of trust and certainty, though the two have sometimes seemed mutually exclusive when viewed from conventional ground.

This is not an idea we are simply commanded to accept. It is an experiment we are invited to try. But it is an experiment in which we are not just aloof observers, but involved participants. God invites us to try putting our faith in him. It is an invitation to put his promises and claims to the test.

A Cloud of Witnesses

The first real steps a person takes toward the experiment with God are almost invariably accompanied by a sense of being near the limits of the ordinary. Even in the process of searching, while still uncommitted, it is common to feel something special stirring inside. This has been so widely noticed and commented on that it has been taken as an indication that our deepest human needs and hungers correspond to this search.

Men and women throughout history who have tried this experiment and put God to the test, and who have come to know him by trusting him, have found their trust growing into certainty. This throng, so numerous that one writer has called them "a cloud of witnesses," have found this trust-certainty so satisfying and so helpful in practical living that they have tried to get others to share their happiness by putting God to the test for themselves. This is how a very special collection of documents we now call the Bible first came to be written.

Many of these witnesses, feeling that they were moved by God, wrote about their communication with him. Over the centuries many documents of many kinds were written and read, and tested in the laboratory of living. Some were stories about God's dealing with people. Some were poetry inspired by visions and thoughts of God. Some were special messages from God, warnings and guidelines and promises, often aimed at particular situations and sent through messengers who said they had been specially chosen and commissioned to carry God's words.

Some of these documents have long been lost, though we know of their existence through references in surviving documents. Some of those which have survived never quite seemed to be as authentic or ring as true as others. Some seemed to provide much clearer insights, and even to possess the peculiar quality of being able to make the sincere reader feel directly and personally involved in a very special kind of communication with God through the documents. In time, a selection was made and the selected writings were collected and circulated.

This did not happen without controversy, and it did not happen overnight. One group of such documents took rather clear shape about the time Artaxerxes was the ruler of Persia, when Ezra and Nehemiah rebuilt the temple in Jerusalem and rallied the people of Israel into a new dedication to their traditional faith. It consisted of the books of Moses, known as the Law; the writings of the prophets who were recognized as authentic messengers of God; and certain collections of poetry, history, and wisdom, which were regarded as deserving the same authority. But even after this group was clearly defined, the right of certain books to be in it was debated by some teachers of the books for several hundred years. The familiar book of Esther was almost left out. It is the only book in the collection which does not mention the name of God. Other books known as Judith, Tobit, and Ecclesiasticus were almost included. The Jews did not settle their definition of which writings were sacred until a special council held in the year 95 A.D. at Jamnia.

By that time another group of documents had begun to form. They were put together by people who believed that God had personally come to earth as a man in fulfillment of certain promises in the first group of books, and to show humanity even more clearly than through all previous messages just what he is really like and just how he can help people who will make a commitment to trust him. The man around whose life and work these documents came to be was Jesus of Nazareth, known as the Anointed One. The titles "Christ" and "Messiah" are simply anglicized versions of the Greek and Hebrew words for "anointed."

Soon after the death of Jesus, the writing started. Collections of his sayings, letters from leaders to the groups of believers forming in various cities, stories of his life and death and resurrection, stories of the activities and teachings of his early followers, personal letters, visions of the future—all were circulated and sifted. Again there were many to choose from. In addition to the now familiar documents there was an Epistle of Clement which was very popular, an epistle bearing the name of Barnabas, a book called the "Shepherd,"

38

one supposedly summing up the teaching of the twelve apostles, a gospel said to have been written by Peter, another Apocalypse, and more. They were left out.

Various councils considered the various books, and the final choices and rejections were not generally agreed on until about 400 A.D. The second collection of books was then added to the first, and the whole became known as the Bible, from the Latin word *biblia,* which means "the books." Many people believe that God somehow guided the discussions and decisions taken at these councils so that the right books were collected and the documents which didn't quite deserve the same status were left out. Others see all the indecision and controversy as proving that we must sift the writings for ourselves as we study them.

In either case, this is the heritage left by a "cloud of witnesses." If the Bible is their testimony, or even if it only contains their testimony mixed with mistakes, its significance for us is immense if these witnesses were really in touch with a real God.

Looking at Windows

But is any of their testimony reliable? Is there any conceivable process by which the Bible can be proved or disproved? The answer depends on what we mean when we talk about proving something. There are two very different ideas involved, and we really need two different words for those ideas. The Bible cannot be proved in the sense of being logically demonstrated from accepted axioms. It simply cannot be done, and all attempts to do it are doomed to ending up as circular arguments.

But the Bible can and should be proved in the other meaning of the word, as an assayer proves ore, as an engineer tests equipment on a proving ground, as a child discovers that the proof of the pudding is in the eating. The way to prove the Bible is in the field, in action. This is not the way a geometry theorem is proved, but rather the way in which the documents were proved during the time of the Bible's formation. The consensus of those who have put the Bible to the test in this way is that the ore is rich, the equipment is reliable, and the pudding is very tasty indeed. This is the experience not only of those who feel that its every word is divinely dictated but also of those who believe that it bears the unavoidable marks of the flawed and imperfect human beings through whom it came to us.

I will not pretend that there are no lumps in the pudding. A quick glance at all the various organizations that claim to be true followers of the one true God and a short look at history are more than enough to make it abundantly obvious that there are plenty of problems connected with the Bible, and plenty of people distressingly ready to fight about them. Even today there is disagreement over the documents collectively known as the Apocrypha, accepted by some Christians as part of the Old Testament but rejected by other Christians and by Jews as not having the highest authority. During the time of the Protestant Reformation the debate over what belonged in the Bible was reopened, with Martin Luther wanting to throw out the epistle of James, which Luther called "an epistle of straw." Others wanted to eliminate the book we call Revelation, or the

40

Apocalypse, and others didn't like the short letters called Second John and Third John.

Even among people who are in agreement on what should be included in the text, arguments develop over whether the Bible is literal or symbolic or poetic or historical or allegorical or universal or some of each. There are further arguments over which parts are which. Still more disputes arise, even when the meaning is clear, over what authority the Bible has for us who are living in times far different from those in which its insights were first communicated.

To get hung up or bogged down in these problems is to miss the purpose of the Bible and of the men who assembled it. A series of divine breakthroughs into human history and human consciousness is what brought the Bible into being, unless it is a complete hoax or a collection of lunacy. The point of it all was to facilitate God's breaking through again and again in every generation into human lives and human relations. The Bible is a series of windows cut in a wall which had separated humanity from God, and windows are to look *through,* not *at.*

When we use the Bible in that way, as it was meant to be used, what we see through the windows is God portrayed as dynamic rather than static, "the living God," present and directly accessible rather than distant and accessible only through a book. A still picture of God is not a biblical picture, and a god who would or could freeze or compress himself into a book is not the great Lord God "I AM" of the Bible.

Through the Bible we also see God portrayed as a foundation, whose reliability cannot rest on anything more fundamental or reliable than himself. When he swears a great oath, he swears by himself because he can swear by no greater, the Bible tells us. The idea that our confidence in this God derives from the reliability of a book is just plain silly. The truth is that whatever confidence we can have in the Bible is possible only if God is real and reliable. To argue that God is real because the Bible is true is to get things completely backwards. What we must say is that if there is any truth to the Bible it is because God is real.

The one true God is alive, active, constantly changing as he relates

41

to us, never so busy or so lazy or so disgusted or so impatient that he would brush us off and refer us to a book. God asks us to put our ultimate confidence in him personally, not in some closed collection of documents, no matter how reliable they might be. This is the message of the documents themselves. This is what we see through the windows.

The Necessity of Choice

The testimony of the cloud of witnesses is, at its best, testimony. The decision on whether to accept or reject that body of testimony is yours. They say that God is all the wonderful and great things I have been saying about him, but we have to decide whether or not to believe it. They say that God offers you a new life, in which joy and fulfillment gradually grow to replace frustration, and which will go on getting better and more exciting forever in a new body after we die. They say God loves us more than we can imagine, and wants us as eternal companions, but that he leaves us freedom to accept or reject this love relationship. God will not rape our souls. He gave humanity freedom, and he will not—perhaps cannot—withdraw the gift now that it has been given. That's why God's messages never overpower us, even when we ask for some overpoweringly clear revelation.

There is something in us which says at times, "Make it unmistakable! Leave me no alternative but to believe!" But we cannot escape from freedom even when we might wish to. We will decide to trust and follow God, or we will not. Not deciding to follow is deciding not to follow. There is no way to avoid the choice, the leap of faith.

Overwhelming, compelling proof, with no lumps and no problems, is not God's method. It may not be possible within the present damaged structure of reality. God does not preempt the regularly scheduled programming on prime-time network TV. He can speak through the creation, and through the Bible, and even occasionally through TV and other human channels and institutions. But we have to choose to listen to him or the messages will not get through.

God can also confirm those messages to us personally, right now, but his personal communication can be missed unless we choose to open our minds to the possibility of such communication. Men can study the Bible and still choose to believe that God is dead. Men can study the universe and choose to believe that it started without any help or that it was always here pulsating and never had a beginning.

In fact, C. S. Lewis wrote that before he became a believer his

43

atheism was based on observations of nature. Materially, the universe is mostly cold, dark, and almost empty. The few places where there is matter sufficiently concentrated to make life possible seem to be tiny interruptions, perhaps flaws, in seamless space. Life itself, where it exists, is short, plagued with frustration and pain, over too soon, and able to maintain itself through its brief span only by preying on other life. Lewis concluded that if there is any being responsible for all this, he must be either unconscious or evil.

Eventually, however, Lewis chose to believe God. Some men of faith have said that they believed God because of the creation, or because of the Bible, or because of something else. But the fact that others starting with the same material can reach different conclusions shows that the men of faith really made a choice, not a deduction. It is quite common to talk of "basing one's faith" on a number of things. But the phrase is highly misleading. Anything based on something else is conclusion, not faith. Faith is the basis for every system of thought. The intricacy and beauty of nature and the words of the Bible may build assurance on a foundation of faith, but they cannot undergird faith. Faith in God can be strengthened by the testimony of others, or by observing the creation as we move toward the point where faith and certainty and knowledge all blend together in an ultimate relation to reality. But the very first thing is pure trust in God, pure faith, pure choice.

That is as it should be, for there is nothing that can serve as foundation for the Foundation. Nature can't do it. Reason can't do it. The Bible can't do it. No combination of them can do it. All these derive from him and rest on him. All they can do is point. Nothing is strong enough to bear the weight of God.

I hope that's a load off your mind.

Section III

A Section Ranging from Dead Ends to Unorthodox Beginnings, All Aimed at Helping You Get a Good Start on the Great Experiment, Perhaps Assisted by Menotti, Mahler, and Michelangelo

An Interruption to Admire Art

Taking a load off your mind does not mean that you have to leave reason behind, or put it in cold storage, as you consider how to pursue your search for truth and the Great Experiment aimed at communicating with God personally. All it does is to correct an unrealistic imbalance. Your mind can come on the journey, but it cannot assert any right to command all the other qualities you have and are. All of you can and must be welcomed to the search.

You can be yourself now—body, soul, heart, mind, strength, and spirit. Hunger and reason can search together, because truth can be tasted as well as known. The heart can join the search too, because truth can also be loved and enjoyed. Now you can begin to experience the full complex splendor of being human, and move more toward the realization of that almost incredible potential.

All of your eagerness and desire, all of your sense of longing and admiration for beauty, your need for freedom and fulfillment, your dreams of swimming in love, your vision of a place where peace is not dull and excitement is not dangerous, your hope to shed the limitations of time and to have a life that does not decay or end— all these and more, every yearning for every good, can come out of the corners of your being into which pain or "realism" may have stuffed them, and search for the satisfaction of your whole self.

God is love and light, and meeting him is like starting new on a life that will grow into all those satisfactions and delights. God is not just the creator of this new life, but father and mother as well. At another stage as the new life matures he is not only the foundation and ground of being, but also the shepherd, the lover, and finally the bridegroom for a fully liberated bride.

All these images are inadequate by themselves, but let them stir you if they can, the whole of you, to a new joy in the prospect of the experiment. If I could stop writing words at this point and switch to music, I would do it. Poets and artists and composers may well communicate more effectively to the whole person than any theologian, professional or amateur. Augustine said our hearts are restless until they rest in God, but Bach's *B Minor Mass* and *St. Matthew Passion* may speak more eloquently and memorably. Many of the greatest works of art have grown from artists' experience of Augustine's insight and their own personal search.

I think of Mahler's *Resurrection* Symphony, of Messaien's tone poem *The Ascension of Christ,* and Menotti's opera *Amahl and the Night Visitors.* Consider Michelangelo's painting of God giving life to Adam, and his sculpture of Mary holding the dead body of Jesus. Look at the architecture of the cathedrals of Chartres and Winchester, Salisbury and St. Peter's. Watch for the moments in great novels and plays, poems and stories, when something extra clearly comes through as the author touches on this universal human search—universal even though sometimes denied and suppressed.

Francis Thompson's famous poem "The Hound of Heaven" has caught the imagination of many, talking of our restlessness as a flight rather than a search, with God actually pursuing us "down the nights and down the days." This is another facet of a reality so vast and transcendent that no image or parallel can possibly convey more than one aspect of the truth. You may have caught something of the call through very different channels—a popular song, some morning's light, the ocean, a snowflake, a tree, or an act of love.

Let them all move you toward God who is our ultimate pleasure, and leave me at this point if you can go on better with them. We are all cut branches, still green if scraped, but on our way to being dead sticks if we do not somehow get grafted back onto our original stock. If printed words aren't helping toward that end, for heaven's sake concentrate on the music, or whatever means God's grace may be extending to you. If you stay with me, I'm afraid it will have to be in prose. But God has the ability to speak even through that.

The Difference between being Champion and being Unique

If God is real at all, the weight of everything and everyone rests on him. If we are talking about anything less, we are not talking about God. To fit the description of Supreme Being he must also be the ground of being, the ultimate source and foundation. In fact, the term "Supreme Being" can be misleading, in that it can be taken to imply that he is only one of a group, one in the category "being," existing in a preexisting and supportive matrix.

Any such less-than-ultimate being, no matter how far above and beyond human powers, would be just a fellow traveler of ours in the space-time continuum, and the question of ultimate origins and meaning would remain a mystery. Such a less-than-ultimate being, even though supreme among existing beings, might be perhaps a marooned survivor from some inconceivably ancient flying saucer, a castaway from some primeval voyage by an extragalactic exploring party. A good many science fiction stories are built around precisely this theme, suggesting that the being we call supreme and refer to as God is actually a mad scientist exiled from another galaxy, or a noble pioneer from another galaxy, or some otherwise explainable solitary representative here in this universe or galaxy of a group that has other members somewhere else.

Dualistic versions of this approach have at times postulated an evil being or force, of equal or nearly equal powers, whose goal is usually portrayed as chaos while the "good" superbeing is interested in "order." Any being who can be fit into such myths would certainly be bragging if he described himself as the Creator of all things, the Alpha and Omega, the beginning and the end. Such a being might have a life span of only five or ten million years, or even five or ten thousand years. Such a being might have died in the late nineteenth century, or be on the point of dying now. Such a being might get tired of this neighborhood of the universe, or disgusted with human affairs, and move on. Such a being might be superseded at any moment by the arrival of an even more powerful being.

Champions don't last. Our local Supreme Being, if that is all God is, might lose his title in some interstellar Superbowl not televised on our networks. If the only god we have is that kind of god, then we are back in the position of primitive peoples with tribal gods, only on an astronomical scale. And who would be the authority to award the title in such championship contests?

Such beings may exist. A whole pecking order of them could infest the near and far corners of this star system, and other star systems. Some of them might have been a part of the history of this planet at some time or other, for all we know, as some recent best-sellers suggest. We might have been visited, and our history and technology interfered with. There is nothing in the Bible to say this didn't happen, and there is a great deal in the mythology of primitive man to suggest that perhaps it did.

In fact, some of the oldest parts of the Bible suggest such a possibility also, and so do some of its apocalyptic writings. Looking toward the future, the visions of John, Ezekiel, and Daniel abound in strange beings with powers between those of God and humanity. Specifically, many have tried to make a connection between the flying saucers talked about in our time and the wheels mentioned in the first chapter of Ezekiel.

Looking back even farther, before the time of Noah, the early part of Genesis includes reference to strange beings known as "Nephilim," or giants, with an implication that they were the offspring of the union of human women with a group of beings described as "sons of God." From the way they are spoken of, it could be supposed that these could have been the basis for some of the Sumerian, Egyptian, and Greek myths, and perhaps all other ancient human myths as well.

In addition to these, the Bible talks about several different orders of beings described as "messengers," or "angels." Some of these are pictured as friendly. Others are said to be in rebellion against God and allied with a particularly powerful rebellions angel apparently known by several names, including Satan and "the devil." Paul, who was as well educated as Cicero or Caesar and no less realistic, frequently wrote about such beings in a very matter-of-fact tone.

50

The Difference

With reference to the hostile group, he warned the early believers of a fight against "cosmic powers," "superhuman forces of evil in the heavens." That is how the New English Bible translates his Greek. What exactly was he talking about? And to what kinds of beings, if any, do all those other stories and visions refer? Those are questions that cannot be answered with any certainty, but it is absolutely certain that the Bible does not present a picture of the universe with nothing "Up There" above our perceptions except a single super being called God. Its picture is much more complex, including many orders of intermediate beings.

If God is really God, he is not just a rival of all these. He is much more than the cosmic equivalent of the toughest kid on the block.

A Chapter not to be Dropped
Part Way Through

When we humans face coral snakes and garter snakes, house-flies and tsetse flies, sharks and dolphins, viruses and super beings traveling from other stars in flying saucers, even angels and demons, we are facing fellow creatures. Their limitations may be different from our limitations, but they all have limitations imposed by their environment and the existence of others, along with the limitations inherent in their own natures. We can weigh whatever knowledge we have as we face such beings and decide whether to fight or surrender, negotiate or hide, kill or tolerate or suffer. Through it all we remain unthreatened in the most profound sense, whether we win or lose, since none of our fellow creatures can reach into that center of our identity which we sometimes call the soul. Our bodies and our minds may be damaged or destroyed, but they were headed in that direction anyway. We are born and we die, and while fellow creatures may affect the timing and the conditions of our passage, it is we who pass from wherever we came from and to wherever we go next.

When we face God, however, if God is real, we are facing no less than the Creator of all beings animate and inanimate. We cannot properly say that he exists in the universe, since it would be closer to the truth to say that the universe exists in him, if indeed such an ultimate God is real. There is a qualitative difference in what this facing means to us and implies about us. If he is, he is our origin and our goal, the first and the last, the one who is before time was, and who will be after tenses have lost their meaning. Our language is hardly adequate even to suggest the qualities of this God. We try words like "circumstances," or "parameters" or "conditions" and find that they were designed for creatures, not for the Creator.

When we face this God we are evaluated by the simple fact of the encounter, and evaluated beyond appeal. All we are is included and surpassed in him from whom we derive, of course, and so we are obviously inferior physically, intellectually, morally, esthetically, or measured by any other conceivable standard. What's more precise is to say that we can't even stand in the same line-up. Our only possible value is the value he places on us; our only possible beauty is in the eye of the Great Beholder. The quality of his existence makes him the ultimate judge. It is not surprising that Solomon, reputed to have been the wisest of men, said that wisdom must begin with the fear of this God, the "wholly other."

All this creates a problem for us. Any recognition of the greatness of God must sound like a put-down of humanity at first hearing, and the thicker it is laid on, the more of a put-down it seems to be. It is quite natural, then, that humanity frequently reacts negatively to certain traditional "religious" expressions, and to much of what is called "worship."

Sometimes people openly resent being made to feel small. More often the response is one of suppression and subconscious denial of the whole issue and the questions it raises. These reactions are easily reinforced by the fact that unresolved psychological problems of the "worshipers" often color their actions and words with unhealthy and repugnant overtones.

But even if we set aside the problems caused by hypocritical and neurotic religionists, asking questions about God can be deeply disturbing to even the most balanced personality. It means simultaneously asking questions, intentionally or unintentionally, about oneself, and few people voluntarily face these troublesome questions. To face God as real is to face oneself from an entirely new perspective. The greater we see God to be, the smaller we must at first feel, and it is easy to feel like nothing at all.

Yet fundamentally and ultimately this is not true, if what he tells us can be trusted, and this makes all the difference. I cannot emphasize too strongly that the real point of this chapter is in these two closing paragraphs and not in all that has gone before. Stopping at the end of the paragraph above is missing the most important bit of evidence about ourselves, the evidence given by the Creator. If reason alone faces the Creator, without eyes to see him as he is or ears to hear what he has to say, we can easily be driven to rebellious anger, or denial and evasion, or a kind of infantile paralysis of the spirit often found in many professing to be "religious."

But if we see the whole truth, listening to what God tells us about the origin and destiny and condition of humanity, we see ourselves as more, not less, than we had previously perceived ourselves to be. The evidence is not all easily available to our senses or reason, God tells us, since we are at the moment damaged, sick, fallen, in a condition from which it is hard to judge what we once were and what we may become. This means that the tragedy of being proud or self-satisfied is not primarily that it offends God but that it keeps us from seeking and accepting the cure, the help, the redemption which he wants to effect. The fear of the Lord is the beginning of wisdom, but not the final wisdom. The despising of self which we are told is necessary is a means, not an end. We have to stoop only to emerge through the narrow door of the prison into perfect freedom.

Who Needs Recognition?

The transcendent greatness of God makes his motives and methods radically different in many ways from what our experience of human psychology might lead us to expect. God is not interested in "recognition." Neurotics need recognition. Unreal gods are often pictured by their priests as needing recognition. People who feel insecure or inferior search for recognition to reassure themselves that they have value. If they can find others who "believe in them" they gain some extra degree of confidence in themselves.

This, it should be obvious, is not the sense in which God calls on people to believe in him, and it does not give us the reason for his asking us to believe. He is not concerned with anything so trivial as trying to establish the fact of his existence. If your concern is limited to such intellectual curiosity, if you have no further interest in God beyond settling the question of his reality for the sake of philosophical neatness, then your attitude is pointing you in a direction which will make it impossible for you to see the true God.

There are people who think they are "religious," and imagine that they have satisfied some cosmic requirement, simply because they include "God" in their systems of thought. But such a tame and containable god is not really God, and the kind of belief God calls for is wider and deeper than the purely rational kind. The reason for this is that what is at stake is real, not just abstract. We are in a real predicament, which includes our mortality, and a real cure is offered. Admitting that we have a disease is an important step toward a cure, but we must do more than stop saying "I'm OK." If we are sick, we cannot get well simply by saying we believe in the necessity and the effectiveness of the medicine; we must take the medicine. Every doctor has seen patients who suddenly say they feel much better when they see the size of the needle required to give the needed injection, or when they learn that an operation with general anesthetic will be required. Unless the patient can be influenced to fear the disease more, or to trust the doctor more, the sickness may destroy the person.

This is why God does not call simply for assent to some propositional statement, but for confidence and trust. There are real issues at stake, life or death issues, not just abstract beliefs. This is why the call for trust comes in so many forms with so many different qualities, sometimes as a command, sometimes a plea, sometimes an offer, and sometimes a statement about reality. The variety appears to be designed both to reflect the complexity of the issue and to appeal to the variety of human moods.

The command form is rare. More often we find the form of an explanation, pointing out that God is the one who knows how the universe works, and warning of the consequences of ignoring his directions. The form of a plea is very common, because God has made us free to accept or reject his explanations and commands about our sickness and his cure, and this leaves him in the position of having to entice and persuade us to our own good. The form of an offer is also frequent, reflecting the fact that we are the ones with the problem and he is the one from whom all the good things come.

Basically these are facets of the same jewel. As a promise or a statement of alternatives, God's offer is to solve our problems, meet our needs, satisfy our desires, repair our damage, and fulfill our nature and potential, if we will choose to trust him. As a request, ranging in force from command to pleading, God asks that we trust him, in a total and continuing sense throughout our lives, so that he can do all those wonderful things for us.

To some of you who are hesitant, such a total commitment—a leap of faith with such intimate and far-reaching effects—may be alarming, like the needle or the operation to the nervous patient. You might be content if you could give God diplomatic recognition and let it go at that. You could perhaps accept God at a reasonable distance. You certainly don't want him for an enemy. If forced to wager, you might play it safe and bet that he is real. Yet you may be afraid of any alliance or treaty which looks as though it might

56

lead to what you feel could be an infringement on your freedom, or even your identity.

But the formalities of recognition alone will not help us toward our safety or our desires, and they do absolutely nothing for God. He already knows that he is real.

What's His Angle?

Just what does God want out of this relationship? It is so common for us human beings to have ulterior motives that it is hard for us to imagine a being whose mind doesn't work that way.

I don't mean to imply that God has no desires where we are concerned. God is not some wishy-washy neuter who gets nothing out of it when we trust him. Certainly he never gives us such a bloodless eviscerated picture of himself. He agonizes over us when we are in trouble and thrills with us when things go well for us, just like a lover, or a good parent. These are the images he uses in trying to communicate to us how he feels about the whole thing. If they sound too anthropomorphic to you in the way they picture God, consider that they might come rather from a theomorphic view of humanity. Don't forget that he tells us that we were made in the image of God, male and female.

A former president of General Motors who had been given the job of United States Secretary of Defense was once being interrogated on the possibility of conflict of interest, since G.M. had such large contracts with the Defense Department. His response was that what was good for the United States was good for General Motors, and that what was good for General Motors was good for the United States, and so he saw no conflict of interest. This shocked many Americans, even some who did not doubt the man's personal integrity. They were willing to see him serve the country in the belief that this would be good for his former company, but there was widespread feeling that it was not as safe for him to consider in his job that whatever he might do to help his former company would somehow benefit the whole United States.

Our knowledge of human nature and human weaknesses was behind the suspicion. Unfortunately this kind of suspicion can carry over into our thinking about God. God gets a bad image because of the way people behave. This is understandable, but unfair. It is a handicap God has to work against, and it is a handicap that his enemies try to perpetuate and exploit with deadly persistence and cunning.

The fears they raise are bogies. We will not be enslaved, or swallowed, or stripped of our personality. God promises us true and perfect freedom. He promises to fulfill in us a potential for incredible greatness, a potential he put there. He promises to join us to himself as his sons and daughters so that we become as close to him and as much like him as he is to himself, all without our being in any sense dissolved or depersonalized. He promises that in this union, which is also pictured as a marriage in which we are his bride, we will not lose our identity in any tiniest sense, but will on the contrary finally find and experience for the first time our true and full identity, which has been clouded and repressed by our circumstances here.

What is God's angle in making his demands and offers? What does he want out of his relationships with us? You might say "absolutely nothing." And it would be true. Or you might say "absolutely everything," and that would be true also. There are no trade-offs involved in trusting God. We lose nothing and gain everything, and it is the same for him. What is good for us is great for him, and what is good for him is great for us. There is no conflict of interest between him and us. Each is enriched by giving. Each delights the other by being delighted.

That is what true love would be like if we could experience it, isn't it? And every time we come close, we get a glimpse of God, because "God Is Love."

The Fabulous Offer

If we can be encouraged by the occasions when we have had glimpses in our experience of something like this perfect love, perhaps it will be easier for us to accept the idea that this picture of God might not be "too good to be true." What pathos there is in that common human saying! We have been stung so many times in so many ways by so many phonies that it is exceedingly difficult for us to believe anything purely good, with no strings, no catch, no fine print, no unpleasant unforeseen side effects. If we could really believe that God actually does love us that way, and that we actually would find all those wonderful consequences of trusting and getting to know him, that belief would certainly have more than a casual impact on our lives.

To recall an image from an earlier chapter, if we really believed that flying saucers were in the vicinity of our planet, carrying powerful beings with the capacity to greatly help or greatly damage us, it certainly would affect our behavior. In West Germany there are two organizations of UFO believers who are so affected, at least apparently, by their faith. The leader of one group insists that the beings in the flying saucers are friendly, and will help solve humanity's problems if we will meet their conditions. The leader of the other group insists that the beings are hostile, intent on taking over the world, and he has sworn out a private warrant for the arrest of the leader of the other group as a traitor, collaborating with a "foreign power" against the interests of the nation. This happened in 1976, and the West German federal prosecutor was faced with the decision of whether or not to take the case to court. He had to go on record as believing or not believing in the flying saucers.

If we believed that there were really visiting aliens, we would be making serious efforts to find out whether they would be hostile or friendly. If we believed that they could indeed wipe out poverty and hunger and the energy shortage, we would be seriously trying to establish communication with them. Our efforts would be as serious, and for the same reasons, as the efforts of nonprofit groups scrambling to obtain grants from great foundations. We would be as active and as serious as poor nations trying to obtain foreign aid funds from the wealthy powers. Genuine faith always produces activity. Faith is never a final step; it is just the starting point for appropriate action.

This is why James, one of Jesus' close friends, made such a point in his letter to the growing group of the faithful about the close connection between belief and behavior—faith and works. One meaning of the word "believe" is intellectual assent to a proposition, but that kind of belief is only a part of choosing to make confidence in God the foundation of your life. "Even the demons believe—and shudder!" That's the way James put it, warning us that intellectual assent is not the same as a leap of faith.

If all God wanted was the intellectual assent, the diplomatic recognition, then men would have a right to question his goodness. Such a hunger has a sick sound to it. What's more, such a limited objective should be ridiculously easy to attain for a real God. A voice from heaven at the right moment, a few perfectly timed lightning bolts on well-publicized targets, perhaps the prominent appearance of a legion of angels, and that ought to take care of it. But what God wants is our trust, our confidence, so that he can repair our damaged world. He wants the deep joy and fulfillment in union which his gift of love can bring, both to us and to himself.

In a way it's as though some fabulously successful millionaire were pleading with us for the authority to handle our financial affairs. I'm fairly sure that if you were to receive such a plea, a plea more reasonably described as an offer, you would have two reactions: You would wonder first whether it was some kind of gag, too marvelous to be true, and second, you would snap it up if you could overcome your cynicism enough to check and find that the offer was genuine.

When God makes the offer to humanity, the offer to adopt us as his sons and daughters, with all the privileges and opportunities that implies, some ridicule it. "There must be a catch." Others say yes, but never follow his advice if it seems to conflict with their own immediate perceptions. Some go as far as to try to follow God's directions, but with a long face and a defeated attitude, saying in a tone of sad resignation "Not my will but thine be done." Only a few believe the offer, joyfully accept it, follow through on taking advantage of it, and try to spread the good news around among their friends that this fabulous offer is available.

In Church or on the Golf Course, and Other Alternatives

Summing up a bit, we can perhaps eliminate a few dead ends. In our search for God, we're not looking for the culmination of a line of reasoning, nor for the champion at the top of a cosmic pecking order, nor for a neurotic superpower hungry for recognition, praise, and worship. "If I were hungry, I would not tell you, for the world and all that is in it are mine," we read in the Psalms. Paul, speaking to a group of curious intellectuals in Athens put it this way: "The God who made the world and everything in it, being Lord of heaven and earth, does not live in shrines made by man, nor is he served by human hands as though he needed anything, since he himself gives to all men life and breath and everything." These are statements that challenge us to lift out sights, and we are not pointed in the right direction to see the true God if we have limited lesser images dominating our hopes or our fears.

To meet God personally we must be prepared to meet one who is meaning and goal, origin and ground, the delight of our dreams and the death of our diseases, friend and father, judge and lover, truth, beauty, mystery, hope, and much, much more. And we must be prepared also to see ourselves as we really are, more damaged and in need of help than we have probably ever admitted before, but also far greater in real essence and potential destiny than we have ever imagined.

But where shall we look for this liberating vision of the true God? Does it have to be in church? Actually the golf course, where so many people would prefer to spend their Sunday mornings in nice weather, is one of the better starting points, though it is sometimes regarded with disfavor by organized religion. At least the golf course is usually a place where almost no one can help seeing how beautiful and marvelous a tree is, and we all know who is the only one who can make a tree. Considering the relative quality of the average tree and the average church, I would often rather rest my case on the trees. And you can try skiing or the beach if you don't care for smacking and chasing that little white ball.

Trees and oceans, sunsets and waterfalls, mountains and the marvels of the human body have many times brought people to the point of encounter with God. I am never surprised to find admirable people concerned with preserving the beauty and healthy survival of our environment, or enjoying the pleasures of getting away from human works and surrounding themselves with nature's loveliest settings. But these wonders do not always do the job of leading a person to see and know God. The universe is marred by the presence of pain, frustration, and evil. Even at its best the creation is not as convincing to all as it was to Sherlock Holmes when he made his deduction from the flowers.

You may recall the argument for atheism which C. S. Lewis made from observing nature before he became a believer. This should not surprise or dismay anyone, for even the first hints coming through from God should have shown us that we can never make his reality depend or rest on the creation, or on anything else.

This gives me courage to suggest that looking for him in church is not to be totally despised and rejected either. It is true that churches are marred by hypocrisy and pettiness just as the universe is marred by suffering and death. Even at their best churches do not convince everyone, any more than the best of nature does. Still churches, like the wonders of the creation, have their record of successes in helping some people to meet God— particularly children, who are often more forgiving than adults.

Reading and studying the Bible can also bring about the personal encounter with God. It is full of surprising bits you might never hear about without reading it for yourself, even though other parts of it are talked almost to death. Try prayer as another possible way to get in touch with God. It doesn't have to be fancy or formal; just talk to him. And look for him in love. The apostle John, a man to whom Jesus was particularly close, once said: "Whoever loves is born of

God and knows God; but the unloving know nothing of God, for God is love."

Try any of these alternatives as you search. Better still, try all of them. And be prepared to discover how true it is that when it comes to God, those who truly seek shall find.

Section IV

A Section Designed to Help Undo
the Brainwashing of Culture
and History, So That You Can Keep
or Find Your Own Identity and Avoid
Slipping into the Generation Stew

The Problem of Trying to Find a Guide

Having considered some questions of method in the search, and some directions, trying to eliminate some and suggest others, I would like to be able to tell you now, in a competely final and authoritative way, just exactly what God is really like. But, to put it mildly, there are difficulties.

I wish I could settle for you forever the questions about where we come from, where we are headed, what God has been doing for the last several thousand years in relation to humanity, and why in spite of his goodness and power there is still a terribly distressing amount of evil and pain in the world. I would like to make it perfectly clear to you just exactly how you can best proceed to get to know God better, precisely what requirements he has, and what kinds of help he can give us with our problems. I have some pretty strong convictions on all these matters, but why should you put any confidence in what I say? Might not all my writing and thought be just another case of "the blind leading the blind"?

There are practical parallels to this problem in our experience. When you emerge from the airport in a strange and distant country, you may find yourself facing a small horde of enterprising local citizens eagerly offering themselves to serve you as a combination interpreter, baggage guardian, tour designer, shopping assistant, money changer, and protector from all the other would-be guides.

One of this horde might beg you to follow him, saying that all the others are rascals who would cheat you. The history of organized religion is studded with that kind of proclamation, often followed up with the enforcement of fire and sword. A guide with a different style might suggest to you that the others are decent and sincere for the most part, but not really as sophisticated or prepared to help you find just exactly whatever it is you have been traveling for. This also can happen to you in your search for God.

And there will be other guides with other styles, and no one to help guide you to the right guide, if there can be said to be a right guide. Similarly there are a great many organized groups, some

69

calling themselves religions and some calling themselves philosophies or lifestyles, claiming to be able to guide you. They offer the path to true enlightenment, to power, to happiness, to adjustment, to health, to self-realization, to salvation, and so on and on, through breathing, chanting, meditation, posture, biofeedback, autohypnosis, ritual, symbolism, belief, or some other formula. To a truly open-minded person looking for ultimate answers, too much help is offered by our culture and our history, and not enough help in evaluating the help.

In some countries where you travel you may find that in addition to the many clamoring guides there is another option. A long established and widely respected best-selling guidebook may be available, reasonably priced or even given away free by the airline or the hotel. You may decide to study the book for yourself, using it instead of a guide, or perhaps using it to check up on the guide your choose. But there may be several other guidebooks offered in competition, and the reliability of any or all of them may be questioned. Choosing one of them is qualitatively no different from choosing a living guide. It is just relying on a past person rather than on a present person, and weighing into the decision some assumptions about those who have earlier made the same choice.

Another approach is to ignore them all, choosing yourself as guide, following your impulses wherever they may lead. But this could get you killed, or robbed blind. It fails, like the others, to guarantee a solution to the problem of avoiding hidden dangers and finding hidden treasures. In fact, theoretically that course might be the least likely to get you to the best restaurants, the greatest bargains, the rarest and most beautiful sights, or even the best opportunities for unstructured spontaneous enjoyment free from hassles.

Still another answer to the dilemma is not to travel. But that could be the greatest risk of all. Every choice leads to dangers and to opportunities, and not choosing is itself a choice.

The Problems of Trying to Be a Guide

Leadership has always been a serious responsibility, and the more critical the situation, the heavier the responsibility. In actual vacation travel, almost any leadership will turn out to be adequate, since there is such a great variety of pleasurable experiences to be found. It's hard to miss a good time. And if you advise people to stay home and enjoy their own back yards, that can be great too.

But if a person is in trouble in Hungary, looking for a guide to help with crossing the border into Austria, through the mine fields and the dog patrols, the problems of an ethically sensitive guide can be as great as the problems of the traveler looking for help. The same is true when the person needing guidance is facing a completely unrecognized danger, like the people on the Titanic ten minutes before impact with the iceberg. Speaking up and offering suggestions in either case is a great responsibility, and so is keeping silent.

In our own time, in completely secular terms, this is part of the burden that makes the job of air traffic controller at a major airport such a tense occupation. Lives hang on every word, and on every pause or hesitation. It is easy to understand how many people would not want that kind of a job, considering how much horror could come from a mistake. That was the kind of thing Jesus had in mind when he warned in his time that religious leaders who lead little ones astray would have been better off never being born, or being thrown off a dock into the harbor wearing concrete shoes. Actually he said wearing a millstone for a necklace, but the idea is the same.

All this would seem to make it pretty clear that it would be arrogant, foolish, and highly dangerous under any circumstances for me to offer myself as your guide in getting to know God, and particularly dangerous in view of the competition from the many available guides. It would even be foolish for me to suggest, on my say-so, that you should listen to no guides at all from culture or history but instead simply search for God sincerely on your own, or just with the aid of one particular guidebook, the Bible.

But there are special circumstances in the search for God which

71

do not apply in the search for other desired goals. The hypothetical situation with the guides and the waiting countryside seems to present an unanswerable difficulty, where the only course open is to make a choice and take the plunge, risking whatever may come even though the choice might in the end cost you your life. The beauties of the country and the lovely waiting experiences cannot call out to you at the airport and help you. The buried treasure cannot communicate with you and your shovel. Mines along a death strip between nations will not whisper warnings to the desperate refugee. In all those situations the goals are passive. God is not. God, being real, can get through to you and help.

Remember the point that God, like the flying saucers if they are real, clearly has the power either to stay hidden or to communicate. If God should choose to hide, no collection of guides and guidebooks could search him out. Such an effort would be even more futile than searching for the UFOs with atmospheric planes and space satellites that can only travel in directions they are thrown, with minor adjustments. The alien visitors could laugh at our jet fighters and our skylabs and our radar and our little laser beams. If they are capable of deep space travel, such things must seem like children's toys to them.

But if God has chosen to try to break through to us, to guide and draw us to where we can find all the good things we desire and yearn for, then certainly he can make himself known and heard over the chatter of the human guides, or through it. If the object of our search is himself searching for us at the same time as we are trying to see and hear him, then he himself will be your Guide to all the guides and guidebooks. This is why I have no hesitation in suggesting that you keep your eyes and ears and heart and mind open for such a Guide. I am merely joining the "cloud of witnesses" who have said, in different words, what Israel's King David expressed when he sang: "Taste! And see that the Lord is good!"

Babble and Silence,
and Must Things be so Difficult?

I do believe that some guides and guidebooks are more misleading than others, and that you should think carefully about the options open to you. Some can scramble your brains. If you talk to God, this is an important issue to raise in your conversations with him. If you are not talking to him yet, it's not a bad issue to begin with, even if you feel that you have to open with a preface explaining to him that you are not sure he is there and listening.

"But if you are there, God . . ." What can you lose? Talking to him that way is from your point of view an open-minded thing to do, so you don't have to lose your intellectual self-respect. And there might be a lot to gain. As the great French mathematician Pascal pointed out, it is a reasonable wager no matter what your beliefs or uncertainties may be. And God will not be offended. He is more likely to be amused. Still more probably, actually, he will be touched by your earnest attempts to be true to what you think are important values, like not trying to con him.

How will God answer? That I don't know. He has an amazing taste and capacity for variety. He has spoken through dreams, through trances, through friends, through strangers coming to visit, through the casting of lots, through a voice from the skies, through special people who were known all their lives as channels through whom he spoke, and even through the mouth of a donkey according to one story. Jesus said one time, when a whole crowd was making a statement of important truth, that if they were quiet God could speak through the stones. Some of these ways are dramatic, and many are not. The people known as God's prophets were often disbelieved even when he spoke through them. They were sometimes honored, but sometimes ignored while the crowds and the establishment listened to competing voices claiming to speak in the name of God.

There is one point, however, which all the methods have in common. Even the most dramatic, like the voice from the skies, never

73

happen in such a way as to overpower the mind or senses of those on the receiving end. God's messages are almost always avoidable. Very seldom, if ever, has he answered requests for guidance by shouldering aside the other guides or shouting them down. Very frequently his messages actually come through them, even through many who seemed unaware of being channels for his insights. This means that you must be interested in listening to the answer you ask for, or you may not hear it. And certainly you can ask him to help you find the most useful guides and channels, and to help you avoid the most confusing or dangerous.

I would particularly request that you ask him to cancel out in your thought anything confusing or dangerous that may have slipped into my own efforts to help guide you toward him, and to reinforce and recall to your thinking anything I say that might be truly helpful. For many reasons, including the one about the millstone pendant, I don't want to lead anyone astray.

It would be difficult, however, for me to do anything more likely to lead people astray than simply remaining silent, offering no attempt at guidance in a culture where distortion and confusion are as bad as they are in ours. Pandora's box is open. Humanity is bleeding from the wounds of hunger and hostility, tribalism and racism, quarrels over wealth and quarrels over political theory, and any kind of help is better than apathy. A truly compassionate doctor coming to the scene of an auto crash, even though he might fear a possible future malpractice lawsuit as a result of his actions, will try to save life if he can. And if there is no doctor on the scene, the compassionate bystander will try, if moments could make the difference, to administer whatever first aid comes to mind from having taken a course or even from having seen some techniques demonstrated on a television show.

The parallel is not excessively dramatic. Today's world doubts its own survival. Every moment without nuclear war is a moment of borrowed time. There are not many left who believe that science and reason alone can solve all the problems. Some experts believe that in polluting the environment we are already past the point of no return. Nearly everyone now is talking about the need for values, and there is a growing realization that we ourselves are the most urgent and the most baffling of our problems.

Even the nature of the problem of humanity is not known, which leaves us far from knowing how to begin to prescribe for our own malady. We are portrayed by our most famed thinkers as anything from the noblest of beings to the most base; from lords of the universe, each comprising a manifestation of "God," to "totally depraved" through original sin, with original sin often tied to sex and sex to an apple. The devil has been made into such a caricature that it is difficult in our time even to be open-minded about how important his existence and activities might be. And God himself? His image has suffered most of all. In a time like this anyone who has any feeling of having any help at all to offer should certainly take the risk of trying to offer it. It is hard to see how we could be any worse off.

It would be nice to have a new beginning, a silent calm, in which the voice of Truth could speak without having to compete with all the winds of doctrine blowing in the air of history. That would seem like a fairly simple solution, which commends itself to any fairly active imagination. Why doesn't God end the babble of confusion, make a silence, and speak into it?

Could God Create a Stone so Heavy . . .

An even more fundamental challenge than the question about why God does not make a silence and end all the confusion would focus on the cause of the confusion. Why doesn't God simply eliminate the necessity for clarity and explanations and guidelines completely? Why doesn't he take sudden and direct action to solve all the problems of suffering and wrong at a single stroke of his power? Why doesn't he fix things in the whole universe so that "heaven" starts right now? Can't he do everything? Why not that?

The most perplexing questions about God presuppose that he could actually do the things which the questions propose. These questions can be asked only if it is first assumed that God is "omnipotent" and can do "anything." But that assumption needs to be examined. Is it something God is trying to tell us about himself, or does it come from misunderstanding? When we study the sources of the Judeo-Christian tradition we do not find God pictured in this way, although it has come to be a part of the teaching of much of organized religion as the years have passed. A partial or shallow reading of some parts of the Bible could be taken as a basis for the concept, but any honest reading of these sources in their contexts gives a different conclusion.

We do find God quoted by spokesmen as saying quite often things like: "Is anything too hard for the Lord?" The clearly implied answer is "No!" But it is from the context that we must get our understanding of what is meant by "anything," and the context is always a discussion of reality rather than of abstract concepts. The Bible is more of a history book than a philosophy text. As such it does teach that God is able to handle all real difficulties, but it does not teach that any sentence constructed to begin with "God can . . ." is automatically true. The senseless and the idiotic do not become true and take on meaning simply by being put into the same sentence with God. Once this vital fact is realized, we can do away at once with such traditional but silly paradoxes as: "Could God create a stone so heavy that he could not lift it?" Nonsense. "Could

76

God make a statement which is both completely reliable and unreliable?" "Could God make creatures who are truly free but also not free?" These are clumsy games, not real issues.

God can create worlds, and he can destroy them and start over, the Bible teaches. It teaches that he can count every hair on our heads and that not a sparrow falls without his knowledge. It teaches that he can make the sun stand still, make iron float, turn rivers to blood, send rain, strike people dead, bring the dead back to life, send plagues, heal the sick, drop food from the sky, make water flow from a rock, feed thousands from a few loaves and fishes, and much more.

But almost in the same breath it teaches that things do not always go as he wants them to go, and that he is often frustrated. All through the writings of Moses and the prophets of Israel we find God pictured as wishing that they would act one way and then finding that they did something else. The friends of Jesus who believed that God was in him, come to earth in human form, taught the same thing about him, picturing him as weeping over the city of Jerusalem and saying how often he wanted to lead them to a solution of their problems but they refused. "Thy will be done on earth as it is in heaven," he taught them to pray, and that is a clear indication that God's will is not in fact done on earth as it is in heaven.

There's no way to deny the fact that the picture of God as immensely powerful and yet often frustrated presents difficulties, and there are more. Can God change his mind? Does he? Where does that leave us? What can we count on? And where does it leave us if he cannot change his mind? What point is there in our ever trying to improve or repent or help or persuade if his mind is already made up? Can God be tempted with evil? Is God all-knowing, or "omniscient?" Can he be all-knowing and still promise to forget some things? Can he remember later what he promised to forget? If not, what keeps him from it? Could he perhaps forget other things, things he once promised to remember? Can God get weary? If he got weary enough, could he decide to cease to be? Could God have created something that might now be threatening to defeat, or perhaps even destroy him? Could he have created something that could defy him and delay him?

77

Certainly these are not the only questions that could be raised in this mood of inquiry about the quality and extent of God's power. I have chosen these because some of them do have clear answers in the Bible that may be quite surprising to you if all your knowledge of that book is secondhand, because they are found in parts that are not often discussed thoroughly. But other questions in the above catalogue have no clear answers, or even apparently conflicting answers, and it would be hard to tell in advance without knowledge of the Bible which questions would be ignored, which would be answered, and which would be controversial. And when we look at our unanswered questions, we must be struck by the key difficulty that we have a serious problem in knowing whether these tough questions are poorly formulated and internally inconsistent, or unanswered because the answers are beyond our capacities of comprehension, or unanswerable or unanswered for other reasons. We are reminded of the necessity of trust, the "leap of faith." Only a being with no limitations will never face that necessity, and our limitations are plentiful and obvious. Among them we must admit our inability to be sure whether we are asking sensible questions. So in rejecting the term and concept of omnipotence we are not trying to suggest a limitation on God, but rather admitting another limitation in ourselves.

Can God make something so firm that he himself cannot shake it? That seems at first like the meaningless kind of question, almost the same as the one about making a stone so heavy that he can't lift it. Yet there is a part of the Bible that speaks of a time in the future when God will shake the heavens and the earth so that only the unshakable will remain. What is unshakable when God himself is doing the shaking? On the other hand, the often asked question of why God allows evil and suffering in the world if he is powerful enough to stop it and loving enough to care, seems like an eminently meaningful question at first, even to minds as great as that of Dostoevski, who writes very movingly on the issue in *The Brothers Karamazov,* in a passage describing a conversation between Ivan and Alyosha about the suffering of children. But in fact the question may be a nonsense question, like asking whether God could create beings both free and not free, or whether he could decide never to have created us free when he actually did create us free.

We may someday have contact with beings from worlds where there is no suffering or evil. But life involves risks, and creating freedom has resulted in this situation where we find confusion and difficulty in trying to know if there is anybody up there.

The Necessity of
Doing Some Things for Yourself

I do not pretend to have settled any of the difficult questions raised in the last two chapters. I do hope, however, that you will be as reluctant now to accept the excessively quick and slick answers of the skeptics as you might be to accept the answers of believers. I hope you will suspend judgment until you get to know God for yourself.

Suspending judgment is often the most sensible attitude to take, and sometimes it is essential. In fact, this suspension of judgment, a willingness to set aside previously heard notions, is the heart of what anyone must do in order to get more than superficially acquainted with God. For while some knowledge of God can come to you through other people, most cannot. God must be encountered and experienced rather than investigated and researched. We are not equipped, either in terms of background knowledge or in terms of intellectual capacity and keenness, for logic-chopping about God or trying to back him into rational corners. That is what we should learn about ourselves from examining these questions we have been raising. What we learn about God, even while we fail to answer many of the questions satisfactorily, is that a real God does not fit easily into our limited comprehension, or neatly into our linguistically limited philosophical pigeonholes.

I believe that the insight and understanding about God's power in relation to the world's problems can be attained, but not through the ordinary methods of learning to which we are accustomed by our educational system. This is because knowing God is not something you can do with just the mind, or even primarily with the mind. You and God cannot get to know each other secondhand, through intermediaries, any more than a man and a woman can love secondhand through intermediaries. Getting to know God is a process that engages the heart and strength and soul as well as the mind, and it must be a highly personal experience. It is not without significance that the word for knowing and the word for sexual union are in Hebrew the same word.

This is not to say that others cannot help. It is not to say that we are back where we started from, with every person having an individual concept which has no meaning for anyone else, and which cannot be challenged since it is strictly personal. Knowing God is not strictly personal, though it is highly personal. In fact, knowing God is the most social of all experiences, since it involves you at once in a totally new relationship with every other human being.

What has long been confusing to generations steeped in the rational tradition is that people who say they have come to know God obviously do not think exactly alike, about "omnipotence" and many other things. This becomes less disturbing when we really digest the idea that the rational is only one dimension of our humanity, and that a real God would have to be far too large to be completely perceived by any one of us in our present limited state. Since our rational views, therefore, are all partial, it is quite natural and not at all upsetting that they are not identical.

If we were nothing more than minds, the situation would be bad. But if after starting to get to know God personally, firsthand, we discover that regardless of our conflicting ways of thinking and talking about God we find ourselves linked with certain other people in shared concerns, in shared hopes, in shared resistance to radical evil, in acting together to help our neighbors, and in many other forms of feeling, mystery, action, and desire, then our differences in the realm of the rational start to shimmer curiously and appear quite a bit less substantial and compelling than the more solid relationship we have as complete persons. This is why "love for the brethren" is far more commonly mentioned in the Bible as a sign of real belonging in the family of God than thinking alike.

And yet thinking is not a trivial part of being human, nor of being involved with God. There will be much common ground in the realm of the rational if we are truly getting closer to God, and the closer we get the more there will be. We are not linked merely by fuzzy feelings when we become part of his family. He will cure and clear our minds, as well as the rest of our being, if we choose to trust him. But this can happen only if we bring our minds to him open, not clenched.

We can get much help and guidance from other people, past and present. All of us have. But whatever we may have received second-hand, either in the form of doubts or in the form of preconceptions, must not be allowed to block the coming of Truth in person. We must let all our ideas be shaken until only the unshakable remains.

Finding Your Identity
or Losing Your Soul

I must make an effort to underline the importance of the need for this willingness to be profoundly shaken. Without it you remain a collection of what has been dumped on you, and you will never find either God or yourself. Only the sweeping away of the second-hand feelings and thoughts will clear the ground for the building of a real personality. Both secondhand religion and secondhand agnosticism have to go, and also that strange combination of both which is the heritage of so many people today, who got some secondhand religion from family and church, followed by a dose of secondhand agnosticism from professors and peers.

Whether the previously heard notions were familiar and cherished, or infuriating and rejected, they must be set aside while you search for yourself. If you do not make the effort, or if your effort is halfhearted, you run the serious risk of being like those of whom it was said that "seeing, they do not see; and hearing, they do not hear." It is suicidal to let the eyes and ears of others, either of tradition or of your own generation, do your seeing and hearing for you. It amounts to abdicating your identity—losing your soul. When Jesus called out again and again: "He who has ears to hear, let him hear!" he was really urging you to shake loose from the crowd and become yourself. The noted psychoanalyst C. G. Jung is urging the same point when he writes in *The Undiscovered Self* that every person "needs the evidence of inner, transcendent experience which alone can protect from the otherwise inevitable submersion in the mass."

We have all been born of history and culture, and we all know we have been marred by them. We have all had our share of traumas, guilt, scars, and frustrations from our tangles with the society. As we wrestle with the problem of finding ourselves and being ourselves, we know at some level that a completely fresh start, being born again, is the only complete answer. But would we still be ourselves? Would we lose remembered joys, or some present real good? Would

83

there be some painful hidden price to pay? Rebirth seems much like death in many ways, and naturally arouses mixed feelings in spite of our deep yearnings for a clean slate.

That is why the question which Nicodemus put to Jesus should never be put down as silly or petulant, but rather should be recognized as penetrating and well-directed, worthy of a man who was one of the leading rabbis of his day. When Jesus talked of the need to be born again, Nicodemus saw the problems. "How can a man be born when he is old? Can he enter a second time into his mother's womb and be born?" The question foreshadows some of the most profound insights of modern depth psychology about the formation of human personality, and it moved Jesus to respond with a statement about the fundamental mystery of the spirit of God and the life of man.

There have been distortions and excesses associated with tent evangelism and sawdust trail appeals. There have also been distortions and excesses associated with that school of Freudian disciples who ridiculed God and faith altogether. Set aside whatever repels you from those traditions and look at the realities, rising above the problems of language and terminology. We have been born of the flesh, and we are corrupted and dying. We want a good life that does not end. God says that the coming of Truth will also be the coming of Love and Life, a new birth. We can and must be born of the Spirit if we want to escape corruption and death. This is the only way to break free of mass-mindedness and find your undiscovered self. This is the only way to save your soul.

Getting Behind Acrimony, Caricatures, and Stereotypes

When we talk about the need for willingness to let all our ideas be profoundly shaken, there can be no exceptions. Specifically, all preconceptions about the Bible must be shaken, because the vast majority of all ideas about God in our culture, and a very large proportion of our ideas about human relations and behavior standards, come directly or indirectly from the Bible. Even the ideology of communism, which seems to be diametrically opposed to trusting God, is actually derived in very large measure from the Bible and from Judeo-Christian cultural values.

Any thinking we do about guides and guidebooks to help with the search for truth will certainly draw us very quickly to an unavoidable decision on what to do about the Bible, and ducking the issues raised by the controversial book is impossible. It must be said at once, however, that God can certainly communicate to people without it. He communicated to Adam and Eve without it, and to Enoch, Noah, Abraham, Isaac, Jacob, Moses, and Rahab, to name just a few. And there have been many other times and places where the Bible was not available. Even now it is not easily available everywhere. So the book should certainly not be idolized or thought indispensable.

But for us, in any society where these words of mine have any chance of being read, trying to ignore the Bible makes no real sense. Being willing to face the Bible, however, creates a whole new set of problems. The Bible is a volume that has been so minutely analyzed, so voluminously discussed, and so frequently fought over, that we can hardly pick it up without seeming to pick up two thousand years of acrimony at the same time. Many parts of it are so closely associated with one rigid system of thought or another that it is difficult to separate the Bible from the traditions and dogmas that claim to explain it more clearly than it can speak for itself. Responses to old associations can be triggered before the words have a chance to be fairly heard for themselves.

85

We are in a position something like jurors asked to hear testimony in a case that has been talked to death in the news media. Getting our minds cleared for a fresh unprejudiced look is not easy. We tend to read the Bible through glasses colored by our experience and our knowledge, and also by our inexperience and our ignorance.

Enemies of the Bible have often distorted its message purposely, and perhaps even more often through never having really learned what is actually in it. But whether it was in order to turn people away from trusting God, or just in order to get a laugh, caricatures and stereotypes have been developed and propagated which have become part of the culture. They are hard to forget, or even to set aside.

Many people calling themselves friends of the Bible have probably done even more serious damage. All their quarrels and divisions throughout history, all their cruelty and pettiness, all their blind spots, hypocrisies, wars, and pretensions start ringing in our minds when we pick up the book on which they have claimed to base their lifestyles and values. We tend too easily to blame the Bible for what they have done with it.

Even a small change of perspective or habit, like reading it in a new translation, may be enough to help us get around some of these problems and see the Bible in a fresh light, giving it a fair chance. For some the putting aside of distortions and seeing through to the real message may be more difficult. But if pleasure beyond imagining is at stake, the effort looks insignificant in comparison to the potential benefits.

Section V

A Section Designed for Those Willing
to Try Giving the Bible a Fresh
Look, Starting with a Reexamination
of the Whole Garden of Eden Thing—
Adam, Eve, God, the Devil, Sex,
the Apple, the Whole Bit

History or Myth, Eden must be Revisited

The story of how this whole situation developed, the ancient Hebrew account of the origins of the earth and God's first dealings with humanity, has been the focus of some of the most bitter fighting between organized religion and its adversaries. Eden began as a garden. It has become a battleground.

Ignoring the stench of controversy, and trying to clear the mind for a fresh look without the filters of either tradition or ridicule, is nowhere more difficult than in the very first part of the Bible. But here is where we must concentrate some serious effort if we hope to shatter many of the false images and distorting caricatures about God and about ourselves.

I will not try to settle the old and continuing argument over whether the first part of Genesis is history or myth, because for the purpose of understanding its message that question is not of primary importance. If the story is history, then it must be accepted as fact and its lessons learned. If it is myth, developed in order to convey some vital lessons, and cherished through the centuries for the wisdom and validity of those lessons, then again we would be well advised to take it seriously and learn its lessons.

In either case, the first step toward understanding it is to unlearn some of the obvious nonsense that has gathered around the story. Very plainly, it was neither sex nor an apple that spoiled the good life in the Garden of Eden. There was not even a "forbidden" fruit in the sense in which we use the word "forbidden." So the "first sin" was not the kind of thing we call disobedience today, even though Paul used that word once in writing about it. I hope to satisfy you quite thoroughly on these points, so that you can approach the story with a clean mental slate.

There is a sex connection with the story, which we will see later, but it was not sex which started the trouble. Far from forbidding sex between Adam and Eve, God had designed them for it and specifically authorized it. When he surveyed his work of creation, including human sexuality, he pronounced it very good, and speaking to

Adam and Eve on the subject he made the famous "Be fruitful and multiply!" statement. He might have said "Enjoy!"

The overt act at issue in the story is the eating of the fruit of one particular tree, the tree of the knowledge of good and evil. Before that act, Adam and Eve were in the state commonly described as "innocence," from the Latin words for "not knowing." They simply did not know good and evil. This is difficult for us to grasp since it is impossible for us to think at all without awareness of good and evil. It is in that sense that Adam's sin made us all guilty. We have the knowledge. We're stuck with it. And with it comes the consciousness of guilt since we have all done evil, even if judged only by our own personal standards. Our whole language is poisoned by our knowledge, and we have no words or concepts to convey simply and properly the quality of what Adam and Eve thought and did.

A fall from innocence followed their act, but the act was weighed and their decision was made within innocence. We must be careful to avoid projecting on their choice our own too terribly familiar categories of "should" and "shouldn't." We must open our minds instead to what the story is trying to tell us, and it goes far deeper than morals.

"Who Can You Trust?"
Ungrammatical but Profound

There may well have been conversation leading up to the moment of the "temptation." There surely was if the serpent was half as subtle as the story suggests. Adam was not there during the critical encounter, and so they may have talked about him. If so, Eve might have reminisced about how thrilled Adam was when he first caught sight of her, saying "This at last!" after no other suitable companion had been found for him in all the creation. She must have been pleased by his delight.

She could not have had any complaints to unload. This was Eden. Pain and evil—including specifically the evil of boredom—had not yet intruded into human life. Each new day, each new vista, each new taste, and each new shared experience she and Adam had, together or separately, must have been joy on joy.

God was not present for the discussion with the tempter either, at least not in the sense in which he came to the garden later, and there may have been some talk about the Creator. That may have been what turned the conversation onto the tree of the knowledge of good and evil. Or perhaps the tempter led up to his purpose by asking Eve to describe the pleasures of the taste sensations of various kinds of fruit in the garden.

Tempting Eve, and Adam, was a very different proposition from tempting us. C. S. Lewis's famous *Screwtape Letters* is a marvelously penetrating and witty handbook on how to tempt humans, ostensibly written by a senior devil to an apprentice demon on his first tour of duty on earth. But Satan, whom Jesus called "the Father of lies," and "a liar from the beginning," had to use different tactics at the beginning.

In the Garden, Satan first had to make a rift between God and the two human creatures, a rift all too real for the rest of us who have come along since then. He had to break down the solid bond of confidence, love, and trust between Adam and Eve and their Creator, who had done everything for them. Things were so good that to make such a rift was a real challenge.

Satan met it with a new invention: the first lie.

The lie started out as a question, and grew into the flat accusation that God had deceived them. Satan's story was that God was in fact trying to limit them, to curb their development and delight, to stunt their growth, to put them down. Satan claimed to be offering them the key to equal status with the Creator—separate, but equal. "You shall be like gods," he said.

Adam and Eve had accepted God's statement about the fruit of that particular tree as a warning. There was one danger in the garden, and God had not left them ignorant of it. They were so happy in their lives that they must have been grateful for the warning, thankful that they had not been left to stumble by accident, through unawareness of the danger, into death. Why should they look at it any other way? Everything good they had was from God, and everything they had from God was good. Not even the knowledge of evil had come to their world.

The conflict, therefore, was new to Eve. God had said the fruit was deadly. The serpent said it would make them like gods. There was the issue. Whom could she trust?

From Trust to Tragedy, Through Lies and Doubt

"Did God really say that? Fantastic! Why, do you know what the fruit of this tree really does? It puts you right up there with him! And he told you it would kill you!" The tempter must have put on quite an act. Eve was sold. "Beguiled," as she put it later. Satan is a master of guile.

So was Iago, in Shakespeare's *Othello*. He connived and beguiled until he had broken the bond of confidence between Othello and his loving wife Desdemona. Othello was a jealous man and did not reject Iago's "evidence" with a confident assertion of faith in his devoted wife. "There must be something wrong with your evidence," he could have said, "even though I can't spot it. Because I just know Desdemona wouldn't do anything like that."

If someone came to you and told you that your mother, or your closest friend, was deviously planning behind your back to do you some terrible injury, you would probably dismiss the accusation as mad ravings, or malicious nonsense. How persuasive would the story have to be to succeed at least in planting a seed of doubt, making you worry a bit? How much more would it take to make you actually believe it, and say with shock: "I never would have believed it!"

The serpent managed to break Eve's trust. She could not possibly have decided to taste the fruit if she had still believed God's warning that it would kill her. She was too happy for that. Before the act of eating, there had to come first a questioning, a worry, a rift, a separation from God, a decision not to trust him. Disregarding his warning was not "disobedience" for her, as we understand the word, with its implications of rebellion. She was deceived. This is the only credible reading of the story.

Reinforcing this analysis is the fact that the whole event is portrayed in subsequent biblical writing as a tragedy to be deplored and remedied rather than as a crime to be punished. Paul specifically says Eve was deceived. A full study of all the biblical references to the story and its consequences could be a book in itself, but even a single

93

fast reading of the relevant passages shows that Adam is held responsible more than Eve for the tragedy, and Satan far more than either. The tempter is cursed; Adam and Eve are not. There are heavy consequences involving them, of which they are warned; but no matter what you may have thought you heard to the contrary, there is no suggestion anywhere in the Genesis story that they were cursed.

The issue was whether God could be trusted, and the question which the tempter raised has achieved a life of its own. Was God really acting throughout in the best interests of humanity, as he and his supporters claim? Or is God perhaps just a bit short-tempered? Is he perhaps really a little status-conscious? If not, did he leave Adam and Eve inadequately protected, and subject to an unfair test? Did he overreact to what they did? Are we all suffering unfairly because of some weird and mysterious rules which he arbitrarily set up?

I would bet that some of those questions have at some time nibbled at your mind. You see, the subtle liar is still at work. Or, if you don't yet believe in the liar, at least you can see that the lie is still at work, trying to keep us from fully trusting God. That was the issue in Eden, and it is still the issue for each of us today.

Punishment, Consequences, Time, and Appearances

If you cut a flower, it's dead. Once it is cut off from its roots and its soil, the channels and sources of its life, it is dead. This is not a punishment for being cut; it is simply a consequence—the act itself viewed differently in time.

If you do the cutting unobserved, covering up the break with your hand or some decorative foliage, no one can tell at that moment just by looking that the flower is dead. With a well-prepared Easter basket, it is hard to tell whether when you peel back the metal foil on the container you will find a living plant in a pot of soil or some cut flowers stuck into a soaked plastic foam block. After a few days have passed, however, cut flowers wilt and you can easily tell that they are dead.

God warned about the tree of knowledge of good and evil, telling the man and the woman that on the day they ate of it they would surely die. If he did not exaggerate, they did die, regardless of appearances. And if he is God, he did not exaggerate. They were cut off from their roots and their soil, and that has affected all of us. The farthest leaf on the farthest branch of a tree is dead when the trunk is sawed through, and Adam and Eve were the trunk of the human family tree. This is why Paul comments on the consequences of what happened in Eden by saying "And so death passed on to all men"; and in another letter "In Adam all die."

This was not some arbitrary and unfair legal penalty imposed on one set of persons as punishment for the acts of another. That would be plainly wrong. What has happened is a tragedy, not a judgment, and it is a tragedy which God tried to prevent. The first sin was a separation to be healed, not a crime to be punished. That is why "separation" is a better fundamental definition for sin than "evil" or "violation of law." Sin existed before law, and therefore cannot be defined in terms of law. What Adam and Eve did was sin, but it was done before there was any knowledge of good and evil, and therefore before the idea of evil or crime or violation of law could have any meaning. It is essential to remember this. The issue was trust, not morals. And the stakes were truly life and death.

Adam and Eve were still walking around after the event, and we are still walking around. But it is well known that a chicken with its head cut off can run around for a few moments too. With humanity the time frame is different, but if the lesson of this story has any validity, death hit us all in the moment of that original breach of trust. It takes a while to show, but we are definitely mortal. The needles don't fall off the Christmas tree the moment it is cut. They look great for a few weeks indoors, or for a few months outdoors in the cold weather. But they will fall in time. One grim humorist summed up the human situation by defining life as a fatal disease. It doesn't have that appearance as you look at the very young, but since the first sin—the original sin—that's just what life has been.

Death is separation from life, and that is what we are told happened because of the tempter's lie and the human response. The first sin, and that is all that "original sin" really means, separated humanity from its roots in God, and the event is aptly described as "the Fall." We fell. The whole tree fell. And that hurt God too. He made us, and he loved us.

"What is this that you have done?" The stereotype reading of that phrase in stern judicial tones, as it is too often heard from pulpits, is clearly wrong. It was God's first question to Eve after her encounter with the tempter, and it could not have been asked in a judgmental tone. How can there be a judgment where there was no knowledge of good and evil in the act? How can there be punishment with no crime? God was not speaking as an investigating policeman, nor as a prosecuting attorney, nor as a judge looking for the facts on which to base a decision. He was not offering an opening for pleas of extenuating circumstances before preparing to pass sentence. That might be in character for some strutting anthropomorphic neurotic, but not for God.

The Start of the Cure

If we search through the Bible for guidance as to what God truly must have felt after the tragedy in Eden, we find it steering us again and again to the analogy of lovers. He was a lover betrayed and rejected. His beloved had listened to lies about him and had mistrusted him, ending up estranged and damaged. It must have been in terrible pain and sorrow that he cried out those words "What is this that you have done?"

God was angry that day, but not at Adam and Eve. His anger was directed against the liar who had caused the trouble. The first thing he did, the story tells us, was to curse the serpent. Then he turned his attention to the humans, in some words and actions which have been often misunderstood. The words have been called "the curse," as though they were an expression of a punishment from an angry God passing judgment for some crime.

But we have pointed out that what happened could not possibly be considered a crime, and the story speaks of a curse only on the serpent and on the ground, not on Adam or Eve. I believe that an unprejudiced examination of the story yields a picture of God in the role of a doctor rather than a judge. Arriving at the scene of a tragedy, with victims who have clearly been terribly damaged, God launches a rescue operation, asking diagnostic questions, explaining as much as the victims can understand, giving warnings, making preparations, and in general getting on with the business of undoing the damage which he found.

It is painful to have a catheter forced through your body up into your heart. But if you are about to die of heart damage without heart surgery, the doctor is regarded as doing you a great kindness if he says "I am going to have to cause you this pain." The causing of the pain is a part of preventing or curing something far worse. We are fortunate to live in a time when medicine has achieved a degree of reliability high enough to give us this example to help our understanding of the scene in Eden.

When a well-trained modern doctor finds a serious illness in a patient and starts a course of treatment, he can often tell the patient quite a bit about what to expect. He may say that the fever will climb for two days and then break and fall. He may say that the swelling will increase and then go down, or that in a certain amount of time discoloration will take place. He may predict rashes, episodes of pain, dizziness, or other symptoms. Some of these may be direct consequences of the original disease, and some may be byproducts of the surgery or medication. The patient is not usually able to tell which discomforts come from the disorder and which come from the treatment, but only the ignorant or foolish would blame the doctor for the nausea and loss of hair which might follow from cobalt radiation he prescribes for a patient with a malignant brain tumor.

This is certainly how we must understand what God was doing and saying to Adam and Eve after the Fall, including the parts about pain in childbearing, thorns and thistles, and even returning to dust. If God can be trusted, we may be sure that he was in fact instantly starting the cure for the terrible thing which had happened, and giving the man and the woman as much warning as possible about important changes they would face, changes they would be better off hearing about in advance from him than experiencing as additional shocks.

Evaluating the Work of a Cosmic Doctor

God, who at first, brought life out of nothing, was now at work to bring life out of death. The reasons for everything he did are not clear to us, but isn't that entirely predictable? We are like Stone Age men watching a skilled mechanic fixing an automobile, or observing a brain surgeon at work. God is trying to cure the human race, and we do not understand either the nature of the damage or the proper healthy state of humanity. The realization of our limited perspective should make us slow either to resent or to ridicule any particular aspect of God's plan. But I'm sure he doesn't mind when we tell him "It hurts!"

If we look at the situation with the assumption that the Cosmic Doctor can be trusted, we are not left with an entirely unreasonable picture. It is possible to conceive certain lines of speculation that might make sense out of most of the story, and to believe that the rest could become understandable if our knowledge of human psychology and cosmic ecology were greater.

For example, the isolation from the "tree of life" makes sense if eating its fruit would have perhaps frozen us in our damaged condition. The undefined powers of that tree could well have presented a frightful danger in the new situation, making it an act of kindness to keep Adam and Eve away from it.

One might also make a connection between some of our modern social problems and the uses we have made of science and technology since the Industrial Revolution, in the light of the warning about our eating bread by the sweat of our brows. That might have been important therapy, and our attempts to evade sweat through the use of technology might have aggravated class distinctions, estrangement from the land, problems of urbanization, population explosion, loss of ecological sensitivity and balance, resource mismanagement, and the international tensions often arising out of these issues.

I am not saying this has to be the explanation of the ills of our time. My speculations along these lines may be quite wrong. What I am saying is that the steps God took can be scanned for either

99

absurdity or meaning, depending on one's predisposition. We are reminded of the inescapability of the leap of faith.

If we choose to trust, we can get some clue as to why God's attitudes and motives in this part of the story have been so often mistrusted. Our modern insights into depth psychology could explain our mistrust quite easily as projection. After all, if we were in a similar situation, with our love and kindness ignored, the seductive words of an enemy accepted and followed, we can all too easily imagine ourselves feeling angry, rejected, and inclined to use our power to strike back at whomever had betrayed us. It's not surprising that we find these attitudes often projected on God. And it's not surprising that we find it hard to believe God's love would still be strong after his beloved lost faith in him and fell for the line of the liar.

But his love *was* still strong. God is not like your average human being. His love is miraculous, steadfast, enduring anything, hoping everything, never failing, lasting forever. This is the most often repeated message, and the most emphasized message, in the whole history of God's communications with us. That is really the whole point of this story, and of every true story about God.

Some Grounds for Complaining to, or about, God

There's a great song by Kurt Weill and Maxwell Anderson which says, in effect, that it seems sometimes as though God has gone away, forgetting the promise that he made and that we're lost out here in the stars! Sometimes it does indeed seem as though the great rescue operation has been stalled, or forgotten. The earth is soaked with tears and blood, endurance is sorely tried, obscene cruelties and exploitations persist, and men of no faith mock that God is dead. Even the most trusting often groan, or shout "Rouse thyself! Why sleepest thou, O Lord?" "Why standest thou afar off?" "How long, O Lord, wilt thou look on?" These are not the comments of infidels and skeptics, but of the prophets and psalmists of Israel.

Any person with half a mind, or half a heart, must wonder why God doesn't clean up all the troubles of the world, if he can. We are driven back to the questions we considered earlier, and we must wonder why he doesn't at least explain why he can't make an instant heaven, or why he can't clean up the mess faster, if he can't, or explain why he doesn't appear to be cleaning up the situation if he actually is. Why doesn't he explain? Why doesn't God end the confusion with a great silence, as we asked before, and then "give us the word"?

I want the silence and the answers as much as you do. So did many of the cloud of witnesses whose writing about their contacts with God have been gathered in the Bible. Again and again, in agony and in anger, they cried out to him in quotations like those above. "How long?" they would ask, and "Why?" For them these were never merely interesting philosophical questions as they faced pain and evil and confusion in their times, but gut-gripping issues that kept assaulting their faith.

It would seem, as we look at pain and history, that either God could handle it and doesn't care, or that he cares but can't handle it. If, however, God is real and worth trusting, then there must be

101

an answer. But when do we get it, and how? These questions are much like the very first and most basic question of whether God is any more real than Santa Claus or flying saucers. They cannot be handled by our normal human fact-finding apparatus. A college student wrestling with these issues in a course on ethics and politics commented in a theme on how education aggravates our difficulties here. She wrote: "Facts are presented with great certainty and pride. The word 'theory' is seldom heard apart from the qualifying phrase: 'only a theory.' The more tangible a thing or an idea is the more trustworthy it is. Questions have answers. All the math problems have solutions listed in the teacher's book, and even the social science questions are neatly answered in red ink. Curricula are gently engineered so that levels follow one another in comfortable succession, and no question pops up before its time. We are thus conditioned to expect answers from authority to every question that arises. Even if the teacher doesn't know, we are assured that there are experts who know. The concept that there are questions whose answers are not clear—that maybe there are even unanswerable questions—is not an easy one for most people to grasp. We are trained to expect clear certainty."

It's true. Students are seldom exposed to the vast realm of the unknown, and it is usually not until a person has accumulated a vast amount of knowledge that it becomes clear how much more vast is the amount remaining beyond the reach of our knowledge. Humility comes hard. Seldom does our culture acknowledge that there are in addition to historical dichotomies some existential dichotomies, to use Erich Fromm's phrase. In addition to the limitations we can plan to transcend within history there are limitations which are part of the fabric of our existence and which we must acknowledge cannot be transcended by our unaided efforts. This is one reason for the fact that our society finds it so hard to face and deal with the reality of death. Seldom are we expected, short of the extremity of being in foxholes, to commit the cardinal sin against human self-confidence of putting skepticism completely aside and asking whether there is anybody up there who can help us.

A new generation is helping us, however, to see through the

pretensions of the rationalists who have answers for everything, or who at least can always see an answer coming around the corner, or light at the end of the rational tunnel. We know from human relations that it is possible for understanding and confidence to grow on a foundation of faith, and we are learning to put more value on personal relationships. We can easily understand how confidence in God and understanding about him could grow on a foundation of faith in him, and so a perceived answer to some of the problems we have about God, though not a rationally convincing answer, might appear after a time to those who have tried to get to know God. But the answers certainly do not come to all, complete and impregnable, in the moment of the basic decision of choosing to trust God. Our faith, like that of the biblical authors, will be assaulted again and again as we get to know God and think about his power and what it might accomplish.

We should note, however, that the whole problem rests on a form of "I-It" thinking, the faith that one's own unaided perception of things is more reliable than what God might tell us. That's why there is always a trace of arrogance in the formulation of the challenge questions, as though we could put ourselves on the bench as judges and bring God to the bar as the defendant. The fact is that our perceptions are limited as we are. For example, they are time-locked, and as we look at the evil which we blame God for not stopping, we might be seeing only shadows of wounds given in a battle he has already won, and in which somehow, in the eventual reality, it may turn out that he was able to transfer to himself all the suffering while transferring his joy and strength to us. In the end it may be true to say that he bore all our griefs and carried all our sorrows. I do not say that this view of time is the answer, but our temporal limitations are certainly aggravating the problems as we perceive them.

The whole situation is a kind of echo of the Eden issue. Do we trust God? The tempter asked Eve to act on her perception that the controversial fruit appeared nourishing, esthetic, and educational. God had said it was dangerous. The enemy said that God was not to be trusted.

Any such accusation is hard to put to rest, as you know well if you have ever been the victim of a false rumor. And if there are some who have an interest in keeping the lies alive, to prevent the growth of love and insight which a renewed trust could make possible, then destroying the lies is even harder.

So what is God doing about it all? It has been reported that he did, in fact, "give us the word," that he sent the Word in person to deal with the situation.

Section VI

A Section Designed for All Who
Want to Know What God Has Done
for Us Lately—Specifically,
How Jesus Fits into the Scene.
PLUS
An Epilogue for Everybody

Like Father, Like Son—and Vice Versa

An old graffiti joke concerns the message on a billboard saying "Christ is the answer!" Underneath someone had later calmly written the inquiry: "What was the question?" We've been looking at some big questions, and we come to one who is reported and believed by many to be the answer. But what does it mean to be an answer to a question? We could understand the claim of someone who said he would *tell* the answer. We would then have the answer to examine. But how can someone *be* an answer? One of the most famous questions of all time is that of Pilate, who asked "What is truth?" The prisoner who stood before the famous Roman official had just finished saying "Everyone who is of the truth hears my voice." But what does it mean to be "of the truth"? We understand knowing the truth, or not knowing the truth, or seeking the truth, or denying the truth, but what is *being* the truth and *being of* the truth? These are strange and difficult thoughts to grasp. They abound, however, in connection with this controversial and unique person named Jesus, often called the Christ, or simply Christ. Who was he? What was he? How does he fit in?

One of his closest friends described him as "the Word . . . made flesh." The phrase fits neatly into our contemporary idiom when we ask for the straight inside story on a situation which is unclear: "What is the word? Give us the word!" Could it be that God did just that, and gave us the Word as the answer to all our most difficult questions? Let's take a long hard look at this controversial person, hopefully with an open mind, and analyze what he and his friends said on these matters.

Among the plainest and most astonishing claims Jesus himself made is what he said to his closest circle of followers the night before he died. John wrote about that evening in some detail, and he leaves the impression that Jesus was talking as though he knew there was little time left.

At first in that conversation Jesus referred to himself as the Teacher and Master, and to God as "the one who sent me." Any leader with a strong sense of mission might use such language. That was not shocking or even particularly unusual. A little later Jesus spoke in stranger terms, saying "Now is the son of man glorified, and in him God is glorified. If God is glorified in him, God will also glorify him in himself, and glorify him at once." If you find that confusing, don't feel too bad. His friends who had lived closely with him for several years were mystified too. They didn't even know how to ask a question that would begin to unravel that one. They just let it go by, since they were accustomed to not fully understanding everything he said, and they waited for something they could get hold of.

Shortly Jesus added that he was going away. That was a straightforward problem, and Peter promptly asked where he was going. When Jesus said "Where I am going you cannot follow me now," Peter asked "Why cannot I follow you now? I will lay down my life for you!" Jesus didn't directly answer the question. He took off in another direction, predicting that Peter's high resolve would not last through the night. Then he launched into a discussion of things they could hardly be expected to understand until they had had a chance to think them over later in the light of subsequent events. His friends had learned his manner, and mostly they just took it all in without questioning unless something really simple caught them and bothered them. When Jesus said "You know the way where I am going," Thomas broke in, showing both his candor and his frustration. "We do *not* know where you are going! How can we know the way?" "I am the way," Jesus replied. It was typical of his mystifying manner, which had so often baffled both his friends and his enemies, prompting people many times to ask him to speak more plainly. They would ask how they could know the truth. He said "I am the truth." They would ask him how to attain eternal life. He said "I am the resurrection and the life." In this particular conversation, he responded to the question Thomas asked by putting them all together in the famous quotation: "I am the way, the truth, and the life." His friends listening did not understand.

A little later in that same conversation, talking about God as "the Father," Jesus said "If you had known me, you would have known my Father also. Henceforth you know him and have seen him." This was clearer, and more startling, but vague enough that its very heavy implications sounded more like a contradiction of common sense than an extraordinary claim, and Philip spoke up to try to get some sense out of all the heavy mystery. "Master, show us the Father, and we shall be satisfied."

That's when Jesus hit them with the big one, and without any indication that he realized what a bomb he was exploding. In fact he seemed mildly surprised that they hadn't understood already. "Have I been with you so long and yet you do not know me, Philip? He who has seen me has seen the Father! How can you say 'Show us the Father'?"

Jesus went on to say that God was in him and he was in God, but many people have claimed that. He said that he did not speak on his own authority, but on the authority of God. Many people have said that too. He said that God was acting through him when he did works of power. Many people have said that as well, and quite a few are saying it today. But how many have said "He who has seen me has seen the Father"?

That is the claim of a madman, or a con artist, or. . . .

What Did You Expect?

Jesus' friends were clearly not able to cope with that claim when he made it. They listened as he talked on, and when he finally wound up he added a kind of epilogue: "I have said this to you in figures; the hour is coming when I shall no longer speak to you in figures but tell you plainly of the Father." A moment later he concluded: "I came from the Father and have come into the world; now I am leaving the world again and going to the Father."

This they grasped, and spoke for the first time after a long period of just listening. "Ah! Now you are speaking plainly, not in any figure! . . . By this we believe that you came from God." Jesus was not impressed. "Do you now believe?" he asked, and went on to predict that they would shortly scatter and desert him.

Even their strong statement of belief that Jesus came from God was far from coping with his mind-boggling claim: "He who has seen me has seen the Father." They had certain fixed expectations and concepts of God which made it extremely difficult to believe that in looking at their friend and teacher they were looking at the Father.

They believed that John the Baptist had "come from God," and so they had no trouble believing that their remarkable teacher, who did such mighty works of healing and feeding crowds of people, had also "come from God." They believed that God had spoken through Moses and the prophets, and had acted through Gideon, Samson, David, and many others, and so they had no trouble believing that the marvelous words and works of Jesus were the words and works of God. But they were not prepared for the astonishing claim that in looking at him they were actually looking at the Father. There were moments when they appeared to begin to get it, but they seemed unable to hold onto the idea for long.

The whole history of Israel was precedent for believing that God could have sent their master, spoken through him, and acted through him. God had sent so many, spoken through so many, and acted through so many. It is not surprising that so many of the people of Israel were prepared to accept this remarkable person,

110

whose words were so powerful and whose powers were so astonishing, as another in the long line of special messengers from God. But they remembered the incident when Moses asked to see God on Mount Sinai and God said no mortal man could see his face and live. They were not prepared, therefore, to look at anyone or anything and believe that they had seen the Father.

They expected that if God should appear, he would sweep his enemies before him. They expected thunder and trumpets again, majesty and a whirlwind. They did not expect someone "meek and lowly," God "veiled" in human flesh, someone who would announce to them that he was about to be seized by the authorities and put to death, and it was within a few breaths of making that very disturbing announcement about his coming death that Jesus had said "He who has seen me has seen the Father." It's no wonder that his friends couldn't fit those two profoundly startling statements together. They hardly grasped either one.

They expected God to send a Deliverer, the "Anointed One" (*Moshiach* in Hebrew and *Christos* in Greek, anglicized to Messiah and Christ), to cope with tyranny, injustice, and all the rest of the problems we have been concerned with. They expected a special prophet to prepare the world for that fabulous event, perhaps a return of the prophet Elijah. Some of the people at various times said they thought Jesus was Elijah, or Jeremiah, or "that Prophet." They saw what they expected. Perceptions have always been closely linked with expectations. The close circle of friends heard the general talk among the people, and reported it to Jesus one time when he asked what was being said about him. "And who do you say that I am?" he asked them. "You are the Christ, the son of the living God," Peter answered, but Jesus called the answer a miracle, and within days Peter seemed to have forgotten it.

At the best, those who listened to Jesus talk and watched him work filtered all they saw and heard through their background of expectations. When he let himself be arrested a few hours after his great claim, his closest followers scattered.

Don't You Know Me?

What does all this analysis of reactions to Jesus and his claims have to do with the issue of whether or not God's great rescue operation has been stalled or forgotten?

Mark Twain draws a picture that can serve as a parallel and make the connection for us in his famous story of mistaken identity. When the prince changed clothes with the pauper who stumbled into the palace by mistake, he wasn't recognized by his own guards. The face was right, and the words as well, but they expected good grooming and saw dirt and grime. They expected silks and laces and saw rags. And the firmness of their expectations made it impossible for them to accept his claims when he declared to them that he was the true prince. Their attention had been so fixed on the majestic trappings of royalty when they had seen the prince before, perhaps at too great a distance, that they had never really gotten to know him well enough to recognize him when the outward effects were changed.

"Don't you know me?" It's what the grizzled prospector says to his family when he returns after twenty years searching for gold in the Yukon; what the lovely young girl says to the boy in the big city whom she used to beat at marbles when they were kids together in a small town; what the soft, spoiled, rich brat says to his mother when he comes back lean and bronzed after two years at sea on an old New Bedford whaler.

The real issue Jesus put to his friends was whether or not they would believe that what they had seen and known when they were with him was actually another visit to the world from God, whom they had seen and known at some distance and through intermediaries before. The same issue was put to everyone who saw and heard him—the common people and the religious leaders, the ordinary Roman soldiers and the sophisticated occupying authorities.

On the whole, the ordinary citizens reacted much more favorably than the leadership. "The common people heard him gladly." An early attempt at arrest failed when the men sent to seize him came back overawed by the things he said. "Never did a man speak like this man speaks!" But the guardians of tradition and morality, of order and authority, found him outrageous and threatening. Finally they arranged his destruction, playing on the fears and weaknesses of the crowd to get their consent in that rejection.

But was it a fair test? Did the people ever have a really clear issue to decide, or any clear evidence of what it was they were actually deciding? Even the authorities could say in their defense that they thought they were acting reasonably in the long-term interests of all the people, getting rid of a troublemaker who could have brought down all the repressive military power of Rome in an area where the hand of tyranny had been light and a large measure of local autonomy had been allowed.

"We never would have opposed God if we had known he was here!" It is easy to imagine that many would have said something like that if they had been unmistakably confronted with the fact that Jesus was actually God revisiting the earth incognito, disguised by the veil of human flesh, the prince dressed as a pauper. "How could we have been sure that he wasn't a fraud? Just a clever faker or some kind of crazy?"

Jesus himself said while he was dying: "Father forgive them; they know not what they do."

113

Objectives and Tactics

There have been so many people who have said of Jesus that he was a "good man" or a "great moral teacher," in a class with Socrates and Confucius and the Buddha, that it is somewhat thought-provoking to note that few if any of his contemporaries saw him in that light. Logically, they couldn't. His claims made it impossible. There is a perennial attempt to ignore or gloss over his claims and patronizingly list him among the world's finer philosophers, but close and honest attention to what he himself said rules out any such verdict.

Jesus could have been insane. Some thought he was, including a delegation of his relatives on one occasion. Another possibility is that he could have been a trickster, a phony using his talents to gather a following. His motives could have been political, or sectarian, or strictly personal. His powers could have been fake or genuine. Perhaps he had some special parapsychological abilities which we are only now in our scientific research beginning to understand. Those gifts could have fed his career as a charlatan, or they could have given him the impression that he was God, creating the delusion that we have to call madness, if it was a delusion. It makes no sense to say he was a sane and decent human being, much less a great moral teacher, either if his claims were false and he knew they were false, or if they were false and he did not know it.

If you don't want to call him either a nut or a con man, you could still avoid a decision to believe and follow him, though. You could accept his claims but charge that the whole incarnation was seriously mismanaged, a bungled interference in history showing either that God doesn't understand humanity or that his aims and goals are incompatible with our desires and our nature.

In *The Brothers Karamazov,* Ivan takes the position, referred to in an earlier part of this book, that he refuses to put his trust in God because God has not shown enough effective power against the many cruelties of the world. He is not so much a skeptic or cynic as he is a critic, and a very morally serious critic. After making that

114

preliminary point, he responds to Alyosha's reference to Jesus by creating the character of a religious leader in medieval Europe who meets Jesus and reproaches him for using the wrong tactics—too much meekness and not enough power. "Thou didst not come down from the cross when they shouted to thee, mocking and reviling thee, 'Come down from the cross and we will believe that thou art He!' Thou didst not come down, for again thou wouldst not enslave man by a miracle, and didst crave faith given freely, not based on miracle."

So says Ivan Karamazov's character, the Grand Inquisitor. But it is risky to criticize anyone's tactics until the objectives and the obstacles are understood. We may never fully understand the obstacles God faced, but we know that in the rescue operation his objective is not to show off his power and greatness. The liar in the Garden of Eden never questioned those qualities. That's why God did not come to earth in force, with the "legions of angels" ready to blast anyone who got out of line. He was not here to win a zapping contest. That's why Jesus so often avoided the obvious opportunities for spectacular action. That's why he so often told the people whom he healed to keep it quiet and not tell anybody. He didn't ever follow up a mighty work by saying "Go tell the religious leaders about that one! Let's see them explain that away!"

Jesus was not here to glorify himself, and he often said so. That's one of the points his admirers often have trouble with, and where the spirit of their actions sometimes conflicts with his.

115

How to Destroy a Liar
and his Lies Together

If someone lies about you, and if you then beat him up or kill him, you have lost the essential struggle. People will always wonder if his lie about you was perhaps true, and your use of power in the controversy will intensify that suspicion and mistrust of you, while tending to make a martyr of the liar, adding to his credibility. You can destroy a liar and his work only by a different approach: you must somehow demonstrate the truth.

This was God's objective, and so his tactics were not the tactics of power as we understand power and as the people of the time expected power. One of the biblical writers explaining the significance of the death of Jesus said it happened "so that through death he might destroy him who has the power of death, that is, the devil." Wouldn't you expect that the interpretation would say that through the resurrection of Jesus he conquered the one who had the power of death? Wouldn't it be more natural to say that the devil tasted victory when Jesus died but was destroyed by the resurrection? It might be expected, but that is not what we are told. The incarnation was not that kind of power play, as we have seen. God did not arm himself to invade a hostile world; he disarmed himself to win the trust of a suspicious world.

In the moment of his death Jesus was wounded slightly in a sense, but his enemy, the liar, was ruined. In the aftermath of the Fall, in Eden, God had predicted this when he spoke of "the seed of the woman." Speaking to the serpent, God said "He will crush your head and you will bruise his heel." For a liar, the truth hurts, and the truth was that God was not trying to keep humanity down as the serpent had charged. In the life and death of Jesus, God let humanity put him down, just to show how wrong the liar was.

Paul summed it up in one of his letters to the young churches several years later. "He who had always been God by nature did not count equality with God a thing to be grasped, but emptied himself, taking the form of a servant. Being born in the likeness of men,

116

revealed in human shape, he humbled himself, and in obedience accepted death, even the death of a common criminal."

The goal of the whole exercise was to lift us all up out of the mess we had fallen into and draw us up to share with him all the glory and power that he had with the Father before undertaking the expedition to earth. This is clear from the words Jesus spoke to the Father on that last night of his life, words overheard and recorded by John.

The issue came into focus again after Jesus had been sold out and fingered by Judas Iscariot. After the arrest, when Jesus was eventually brought before Pilate, the Roman governor, Pilate asked whether he was a king, as some had accused him of claiming to be. "My kingdom does not belong to this world," Jesus replied. "If it did, my followers would be fighting to save me from arrest . . ." "You are a king, then?" Pilate asked. Jesus answered: " 'King' is your word. My task is to bear witness to the truth. For this I was born; for this I came into the world . . ."

The liar in Eden had implied that God didn't want humans to share his status. He insinuated that God told them the tree was deadly just to keep them down, inferior, and in his power. He promised that eating the fruit, learning about good and evil, would make humanity "like gods." He offered, in effect, separate but equal status.

Jesus came and said that he came from God, that he spoke for God, that whoever had seen him had seen God, and that he would willingly put himself in our power in order to get across the fundamental truth that God is nothing like what the liar suggested. Jesus described God as a loving Father. He forgave sins in God's name, went around doing good in God's name, and asked us all to believe that the Father himself loves us. Furthermore he promised anyone who would trust him that they would live forever, and in fact become fully one with him and the Father in the same way that he and the Father were one. That's better than separate but equal status, and that's the prognosis based on the cure we are offered.

Why Does it all Take so Long?

Jesus once told a story which suggests that the whole struggle with evil was intended to be wrapped up long ago, even before his birth. There was a man with a vineyard, he said, who left some people in charge of it and from time to time sent them messengers, with advice on how to care for it and requests for some share of the fruit. The messages were ignored and the messengers mistreated. Finally, Jesus said, the owner "sent his son to them, saying, 'They will respect my son.' "

The story indicates that the sending of the son was a kind of last resort in the rescue operation, something God had hoped might be avoided, and which he expected might turn out quite differently from the way it did. The story should also make it clear that Jesus did not regard himself as the founder of a new religion but as the climax of a long series of actions taken by the one true God. Certainly Jesus never intended that any group of people should call themselves "Christians" or "Jesus people."

Some who have professed to be his followers have often seemed to put him in competition with the God of Abraham, Isaac, Jacob, and Moses, the God who said "Hear O Israel, the Lord is one!" Such a competition seems to me wrong in its essence and tragic in its consequences, and Jesus did nothing himself to encourage such a conflict. He identified himself fully with the God of Abraham, many times and in many ways. "Before Abraham was, I AM!" he once said, and spoke to the Father about his life with the Father before the world was. What is at stake is not Jesus versus "Yahweh" but how to answer our opening questions as to whether God is real and what he is like. Is the one true God a being who can be both Father and Son, and did he come to earth "veiled in flesh" as a baby?

Jesus said that a decision to trust him was a decision to trust the Father, and that in trusting him we would be "born again," started on a new life that would have no end, and saved from all the consequences of our original separation from the Father. He forgave, he invited, he offered, he healed, he fed the hungry. He let himself be taken, arrested, beaten, tormented, mocked, and killed. Would you believe a God who would go to such lengths to prove he is not the distant and fearsome tyrant most people thought he was?

But he did not offer instantaneous time-destroying solutions. He offered a kind of birth, which implies a process. Being born is not the same as getting to know your parents, and being "born again" is not the same as getting to know God. Birth is a decisive change, but mostly in potential. The birth image emphasizes strongly the need for growth. It stresses the fact that the first decision to trust God and accept the fabulous offer is only a starting point and not something to be regarded as a mark of having attained the prize or having reached the goal.

Falling in love is another image we are given of the new beginning, and that also implies process. It can happen suddenly, or gradually, but you do not know a person after the first encounter. The full beauty and depth of the person, the rich excitement and variety of knowing each other, grow as the relationship grows, and the first experience is only a pale shadow of what can eventually develop. The same is true of our encounter with God.

Still the beginning is vital. The decision to trust is the first step in this journey of a thousand miles, and we are told that our choices have an impact not only on ourselves but also on how much longer the struggle with pain and unpleasantness will drag on.

In Closing, Good News and Bad News

We are now near the end of this discussion of beginnings, and I must emphasize again that if God is real, beginning to get to know him is a launching pad as much as it is a harbor. There is an eternity ahead for your environment, and an infinity inside you to be developed, if you come into the safety of this harbor—or risk the adventure of this launching pad.

Where will it all end? It won't. Only evil and all its consequences and side effects will end. And it is interesting to note that this bright view of our future is something that follows necessarily from the gloomiest aspects of our most remote past.

One part of the Eden story about which there can be no misunderstanding or contradiction is that it connects a great deal of the unpleasantness of the human condition, throughout our time on this planet, to the fall from trust. It says that fear came from the end of the easy closeness with God, and man said for the first time "I was afraid!" Sexual freedom disappeared, to be replaced by shame. The perfect relationship between man and woman collapsed, to be replaced by male rule. Pain was to enter the picture, as a part of childbearing. Toil and sweat were introduced, as prerequisites for survival. A return to dust suddenly stood as a limit to life, guaranteeing that whatever good might be found in experience would certainly come to an abrupt end.

But this is good news as well as bad news. All these changes are pictured as tragedies, unnatural and unintended in the original created design. All are pictured as disruptions, digressions brought about either directly, by the breaking of the total trust that had linked us to God, or indirectly, as necessary parts of the cure. The good news is, therefore, that sexual inhibitions, patriarchy, pain, toil, fear of God, and even death are not permanent features of being human. Things were not meant to be that way, and will not always remain that way. The final defeat of the serpent is flatly predicted in God's curse, and that defeat is connected with a human instrumentality described as the seed of the woman.

120

In Closing, Good News and Bad News

Our place in the struggle is plain from the language of the curse on the serpent, where God lines humanity up with himself on one side of a cosmic war and identifies the enemy on the other side as the lying tempter. Our enemy is the serpent, not God. "I will put enmity between you and the woman," God says to the liar, "and between your seed and her seed." With the woman and her seed identified as God's ally and instrument in the conflict, it certainly would make no sense for God to turn and curse her and her mate, and he didn't. He turned to cure, not to curse, and the ultimate victory had already been promised. The serpent had already been told flatly that he would be crushed. Evil will be wiped out. Pain and sorrow will end. Good will triumph and flourish. It is just a matter of time.

The person who trusts God's prediction regarding the final and total defeat of evil will not have to "accept" or "adjust" to evil as though it were part of God's design. There is no need for the rather pathetic, though perhaps brave, statements like: "I suppose it's good we have sickness so we can appreciate health," or "I guess sorrow is necessary to make us appreciate joy." No. Evil is neither necessary nor good, in any form. It is not part of the character of evil but part of the *defeat* of evil that we can turn it into good things, like appreciation. Evil is the enemy, and it has already lost the decisive battle. Choosing to trust God not only puts you on the nice team but on the winning team. That's part of the good news.

Epilogue for Everybody,
Touching on Some Big Words

Everybody knows that three of the biggest words in the whole discussion of God are faith, hope, and love. This book has been mostly about faith, looking at the issues involved in deciding whether or not you might want to put your faith in a real God. But you saw, I'm sure, as we got to the end, that hope would certainly come charging into the thoughts and attitudes of anyone making that decision and finding that if there is a real God there is certainly only one, one who is trying to rescue and cure us, one who offers us present help and a fabulous future destiny.

Love, in this picture, has two aspects. Love is the new law, replacing the old law by being the complete fulfillment of that law, or of any law. Love is the new commandment. But it is also a fruit of the new life, and this is important because a commandment from God would be horrifying if we had no way of doing it. This difficulty is solved by God's promise to help us in a way which is quite impossible to describe briefly, but which involves his own presence in us. The first "fruit" of this presence, we are told, is love, followed by joy, peace, and some other good big words.

I do not regard any of this as religion. I regard it as reality. Religion is a big word but an odd word, of uncertain origin. If it means only some part or facet of life, it is really meaningless and can be ignored. We can therefore go back to looking at life whole, at reality, and the big words we have to deal with in the real world.

History and time are nothing more than the framework within which God is trying to win back our trust. When limits go, they will go. Life is a big word, but life now is only a shadow of what it was, and of what it is intended to be. Death is the last enemy, and it will be destroyed. In the meanwhile, until that is accomplished, death will be made to serve throughout history as the gate by which we pass from this damaged life into a new and perfect life. For those who trust God, this gate has the marvelous property as you get

122

closer to it of looking less and less like an exit and more and more like an entrance.

Evolution? It may or may not have been the method by which God formed humanity and the other beings with us on this planet. It may or may not survive the attacks which new secular science, as it is currently understood and generally taught, is already bringing to bear on it. In any case, it is certainly not the great issue at stake as we consider the first part of the Bible.

Sin is our separation from God. Salvation is simply his plan to rescue us, save us, from the death which that separation entailed; it is his plan to graft us back into our real roots and share his own nature with us. Science remains a fine method for knowing what is beneath us, but it is useless for understanding higher things. Sex requires a book to itself, but the outlines are already visible. Destiny is a happy surprise, coming.

Desire will be fulfilled. In all its myriad forms it is, at its root, a reminder God has planted in us that there is more than what we see, far more than we normally settle for. We are made for more. We are made for the infinite. Don't be too easily pleased. Cherish desire. Search deep in yourself to get in touch with your true desires. If you hunger for the infinite, you will be filled. God challenges us to think of the highest that we dare ask or imagine, and promises to do so much better, and so much more, that when we see it we will shout with the joy of children.